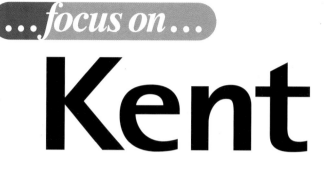

...*focus on*...

Kent

AA Publishing

Produced by AA Publishing

First published 1997

Published by AA Publishing (a trading name of Automobile
Association Developments Limited, whose registered office is
Norfolk House, Priestley Road, Basingstoke, Hampshire RG24 9NY;
registered number 1878835).

ISBN 0 7495 1493 0

A CIP catalogue record for this book is available from the
British Library.

Designer: Jo Tapper

Colour separation by BTB, Digital Imaging, Whitchurch, Hampshire

Printed and bound by George Over Ltd, Rugby

KENT

Kent's reputation as 'the Garden of England' grew from its fertile green fields and orchards feeding London, and its closeness to the capital encouraged wealthy Londoners to build themselves country retreats in Kent, from moated and idyllic Ightham Mote to the princely splendours of Knole.

Armies of middle-class London commuters have their homes in the county today and Greater London has swallowed a sizeable helping of western Kent. The county is the nearest part of England to the mainland of Europe and the flow of incoming people and ideas, and stands astride the main routes between London and the Continent. Julius Caesar landed in Kent in 55 BC. The invading Roman army in the 1st century AD established its main base in Kent, at Richborough, where Herculean Roman walls stand to this day, and the Romans built the main road from Dover to London.

Hengist and Horsa, leaders of the Saxons, landed in Kent in the 5th century in Pegwell Bay, according to tradition, and so did St Augustine and his party of missionaries from Rome in 597. They made for Canterbury, which is still a magnet for visitors with its magnificent cathedral, the mother church of Anglican Christianity.

The Pilgrim's Way footpath to Canterbury follows the long ridge of the North Downs, which cross the county in the north above the M2 motorway. To the south in the shelter of the downs lies the countryside of the Weald with its neat little towns and villages, its hop-gardens and oasthouses, its time-honoured amicable pubs. In the far south-west the wet, flat, cattle-grazed country of Romney Marsh is agog with romantic tales of smugglers. Along the coast, Dover Castle, high above the ferry port and the famous white cliffs, stares watchfully across the heaving sea to France, and Kent's other main passenger and commercial ports for the Continent are Folkestone, where the Channel Tunnel comes ashore, Ramsgate and Sheerness. Maidstone is the county town. Margate made its reputation as a brash and breezy resort for Londoners on the spree, Tunbridge Wells, in upper-crust contrast, as a smart spa. Chatham's historic dockyard is enthralling and Rochester, with England's second cathedral, exudes dignified charm.

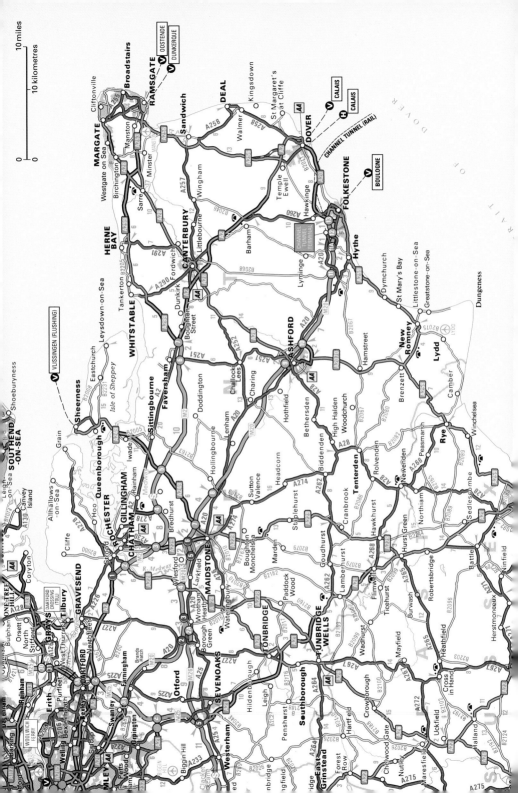

*G*azetteer

This scattered village, set in wooded undulating country, has a cruciform church containing 13th-century painted woodwork salvaged from Canterbury Cathedral.

ADISHAM
VILLAGE OFF B2046, 3 MILES (5KM) SW OF WINGHAM

Set on higher land west of Romney Marsh, this dispersed village, where Erasmus the Dutch humanist was rector in 1511, has a Tudor church tower. Aldington Knoll was the site of a Roman beacon.

ALDINGTON
VILLAGE OFF B2067, 6 MILES (9.5KM) W OF HYTHE

This seaside village is set on wide open land on the north-east tip of the Hoo peninsula near the mouth of the River Thames. The 12th-century All Saints' Church has a richly moulded south doorway.

ALLHALLOWS
VILLAGE OFF A228, 8 MILES (13KM) NE OF ROCHESTER

The village lies on a great bend of the River Medway and has a romantic-looking medieval castle which was built to guard this strategic point. The castle has had an eventful history that converted it from a 13th-century fortress to a grand Tudor mansion, a farmhouse, a stately home and finally a convent for Carmelite nuns.

    The first castle on this site was raised in the 11th century, and was probably only a simple mound with a wooden structure on the top. A stone castle was built by Stephen of Penchester, under a licence granted by Edward I in 1281; the oldest part of this early building which survives is a section of wall with a distinctive herringbone pattern. The castle was converted into a mansion in the 15th century, but a serious fire in about 1600 left only enough of the mansion to make a farmhouse. Early in the 20th century, Allington was restored by the British traveller Sir Martin Conway, who was particularly well known for his explorations in the Arctic. The castle was taken over by the Carmelite order in 1951 and is not generally open to the public.

ALLINGTON
VILLAGE OFF A20, 2 MILES (3KM) NW OF MAIDSTONE

CONTACT THE TOURIST INFORMATION CENTRE, MAIDSTONE, TEL: 01622 602169 FOR DETAILS OF OCCASIONAL SPECIAL EVENTS AT ALLINGTON CASTLE

This peaceful village on the edge of Romney Marsh was once a port on the estuary of the River Rother, but in the 13th century violent storms changed the course of the Rother and gradual silting-up left Appledore 8 miles (13km) or so inland. Not far enough, however, to escape a raid by the French in 1380 during which they burned the 13th-century church. Its chunky tower survived and the rest was reconstructed shortly afterwards. In 1381 Wat Tyler, leader of the Peasant's Revolt, attacked Horne's Place, a 14th-century farmhouse with a gem of a private chapel. More peaceful days followed, and markets and a fair licensed by Edward III were held in its broad, grassy main street. In 1804 there was the threat of an invasion by Napoleon, and the Royal Military Canal was built, curving around the marsh. Today, Appledore lies quietly to the north of the canal, most of it along the main street, its buildings a mix of styles and ages from the 16th century onwards.

APPLEDORE
VILLAGE ON B2080, 5 MILES (8KM) SE OF TENTERDEN

ASH
*VILLAGE ON A257, 3 MILES
(5KM) W OF SANDWICH*

This is a pleasant old village of brick, tile and timber with some modern housing. The tall copper church spire has long been a navigational mark for seamen.

ASHFORD
*TOWN ON A20, 19 MILES
(30.5KM) SE OF MAIDSTONE*

Situated at the confluence of the East and Great Stour, Ashford is an important touring and shopping centre. Medieval, Tudor and Georgian houses have survived, despite development.

AYLESFORD
*VILLAGE OFF A20, 3 MILES
(5KM) NW OF MAIDSTONE*

There is a record of a bridge spanning the Medway at Aylesford in 1287. In the 14th century this was replaced by the Kentish flagstone bridge that survives today. The view from this bridge is one of the best there is of the picturesque brick-and-half-timbered, steeply gabled cottages. The river once powered the paper mill that has operated here since the turn of the century. On the outskirts is Kit's Coty House, the awe-inspiring remains of a Neolithic burial chamber. In AD 455 the Britons were defeated in battle here by Jutish invaders, and in 893 the Danes were seen off by King Alfred, while in 918 Edmund Ironside routed Canute and the Vikings. Later, the Carmelites came to England and founded their first friary in this country in Aylesford, in 1240.

Aylesford is on the banks of the Medway, a little-known but attractive waterway

Built in the 13th and 14th centuries and then closed down in the Reformation, the priory has since been restored and is now a house of prayer, guesthouse, conference centre and a place of pilgrimage and retreat. It has fine cloisters, and there are displays of sculpture and ceramics by modern artists and potters. A potter and an upholsterer have workshops at The Friars and visitors are welcome to watch them at work.

Open all year, daily.

This is a remote, pretty village with a remarkable Norman church of 1080, arguably the best in England. The magnificent, sometimes bizarre carvings, especially over the south doorway, are reminiscent of Rochester Cathedral. They are said to be by Adam de Port.

This pleasant little village, which nestles in the beautiful Elham Valley, has attractive brick and timber-framed houses and a restored windmill. At the Elham Valley Vineyards, to the south at Breach, visitors can take a look around the vineyards and see the vines growing in the sheltered valley, and then taste the wines.

Aylesford Priory
The Friars
Tel: 01622 717272

BARFRESTON
Hamlet off A256, 6 miles (10km) NW of Dover

BARHAM
Village off A2, 6 miles (9.5km) SE of Canterbury

*T*he High Weald presents a countryside of patchwork fields, hedges and woodlands, with steep-sided valleys giving dramatic views of rolling slopes. This ride takes in the romantic historic sights of Bayham Old Abbey and Scotney Castle. Bedgebury Forest and Pinetum give you an opportunity to get away from the roads and enjoy the quietness and beauty amongst exotic trees. But take great care when cycling along the short section of the A21.

INFORMATION

Total Distance
19 miles (30.5km), including
5 miles (8km) off-road

Difficulty
Moderate

OS Map
Landranger 1:50,000 sheet 188
(Maidstone & Weald of Kent)

Tourist Information
Royal Tunbridge Wells,
tel: 01892 515675

Cycle Hire
Bewl Bike Hire, Bewl Water,
tel: 0860 386144

Nearest Railway Station
Wadhurst (4 miles/6.5km)

Refreshments
Many pubs along the route,
including Elephant's Head at
Hook Green, with family garden;
The Swan at Lamberhurst Down
and the Globe and Rainbow at
Kilndown, also with family
garden. Kiosk facilities at Bewl
Water Visitor Centre, Bayham
Old Abbey and Bedgebury
Pinetum. Tea rooms/restaurant at
Lamberhurst Vineyards. There are
picnic spots at Scotney Castle,
Bayham Abbey ruins and at
Bedgebury Pinetum.

*Bedgebury Pinetum houses the
national collection of conifers*

START

Bewl Water lies 15 miles (24km) south-east of Royal Tunbridge Wells in the heart of the Kent and Sussex High Weald. The ride starts from the visitor centre car park, accessed from the A21, 2 miles (3km) south of Lamberhurst.

DIRECTIONS

1. Follow the 'Exit' signs out of the car park. When you rejoin the lane turn left past a low barrier and follow the narrow lane, designated as 'restricted access'. After a short climb do not miss the view over Bewl Water on the left. After 1 mile (1.5km) keep right when the lane feeds into another from the left. Follow a long gradual descent for 2 miles (3km) past Bartley Mill fishery and cross a bridged stream.

2. Turn right for a short climb to the B2169, then right again, signposted 'Lamberhurst'. Continue for 1 mile (1.5km) past the turning for Bayham Abbey Lake and take the next drive on the left, signposted 'Bayham Old Abbey Ruins'. Return via the same drive back to the B2169 and turn left towards Lamberhurst. Proceed through Hook Green, past the Elephant's Head, continuing for 1½ miles (2.5km) beside vineyards to Lamberhurst Down. At The Swan pub turn left for the entrance to Lamberhurst Vineyards, or continue straight across the crossroads to meet the A21. Opposite is the driveway to

Bewl Water

Scotney Castle (NT), which is well worth a visit, but take care crossing the busy A21.

3. Return via the same driveway back to the A21 from the castle car park and turn left. Climb the long gradual ascent for 1½ miles (2km), turn left again for Kilndown and enter the village to view the old Christ Church. Continue for 110yds (100.5m) and turn right at the Globe and Rainbow Inn. The road soon bends sharply left and then meanders for 2 miles (3km) to Bedgebury Cross. At the T-junction with the B2079 turn right and continue for 1 mile (1.5km) to the car park entrance of Bedgebury Pinetum.

WHAT TO LOOK OUT FOR

Bewl Water provides a haven for wintering wildfowl, especially large numbers of tufted duck and pochard during hard weather. Passage migrants during spring and autumn include waders such as greenshank and sandpipers. Late autumn is a good time to see ospreys 'stocking up' on their return flight to Africa. Hawfinches are a speciality at Bedgebury Pinetum; they are best identified by their call as they tend to keep to the tree-tops, making them elusive. In spring the hedgerows abound with primroses, lady's smock, celandines and, later, bluebells. During autumn the pinetum has a rich variety of rare and beautiful fungi.

4. Leaving the Pinetum car park turn right and retrace your tracks for 400yds (366m). Turn right on to the next driveway, marked 'Private Road'. Follow this bridleway downhill to the lake at the bottom, stopping for a few moments to take in the tranquil mood of Marshall's Lake. Proceed uphill until the drive turns into a rough track, continuing past Park House on the right and the Forestry Commission buildings on the left. Take the right fork of the bridleway (not straight on) and follow blue waymarkers. The track continues around the perimeter of the Pinetum, overlooking the wealth of shapes and colours of the tree collection. As you enter a dense pine plantation the track forks; keep left and continue for a short distance up to open terrain. Keep right and follow the blue arrows. Continue on the main track over a ramp to rejoin a tarmac drive leading to the A21

opposite Godfrey's Diner. Turn left and then right at the traffic lights on to the B2087, signposted 'Ticehurst'. Continue for 1½ miles (2km) and turn right into Rosemary Lane, which becomes a causeway across one leg of Bewl Water, a good viewpoint and stop-off. At the end of the road turn left back on to the A21 and continue for about 2 miles (3km) to the entrance road on the left, signposted 'Bewl Water'. Now follow the lane back to the visitor centre car park.

5. The road continues along a 2-mile (3-km) descent into Wye. Follow the 'P' signs past the church to return to the car park and starting point.

PLACES OF INTEREST

Bewl Water

This is a large flooded valley providing many associated

watersports – fishing, sailing and windsurfing among others. It also has good nature trails around the perimeter, providing access for bird-watchers and walkers. Close to the main car park is a visitor centre with a restaurant, information desk and a playground.

Bayham Old Abbey Ruins and House

Situated in the picturesque wooded valley of the River Teise,

this impressive abbey was built in the 13th century by Premonstratensian monks from France. In the 18th century the remaining ruins that survived the Reformation were landscaped to provide a romantic view from Bayham Old Abbey House.
(See also page 46.)

Bedgebury Pinetum
The national conifer collection was started by the Forestry Commission and Kew Gardens during the 1920s and now provides a beautiful landscape in which to wander amongst exotic trees with a rich variety of shapes and colours.
(See also page 12.)

Lamberhurst Vineyards
Established in 1972, there are guided tours of the vineyards, winery and cellars to see the fascinating wine-making process, from vine to glass. The tour finishes with an opportunity to

Scotney Castle

taste the wines seen in production and a chance to buy the product.

Scotney Castle
A National Trust estate with the ruins of a moated 14th-century castle surrounded by picturesque landscaped gardens, this is well worth a visit. Rhododendrons, azaleas, water lilies and wisteria all flower in profusion.
(See also page 46.)

BEDGEBURY FOREST

WOODLAND OFF B2079, S OF GOUDHURST

This large (2,500 acres/1,012ha) area of forest run by the Forestry Commission is popular with walkers and picnickers. It includes Bedgebury Pinetum, home of the national collection of specimen conifers hardy in Britain, established in 1925 by the Forestry Commission and the Royal Botanical Gardens, Kew. In spring colourful rhododendrons add to the collection's beauty. There are nature trails, picnic areas and visitor facilities, and a programme of organised outings.

(See also Cycle ride: Bewl Water and the High Weald, page 8.)

BEKESBOURNE

VILLAGE OFF A2, 3 MILES (5KM) SE OF CANTERBURY

The village consists of a lovely group of old buildings around the church. Howletts Wild Animal Park is near by.

Howletts Wild Animal Park

OFF A257

TEL: 01227 721286

Howletts is one of John Aspinall's wild animal parks and has the world's largest breeding gorilla colony in captivity. It also has tigers, small cats, free-running deer and antelope, snow leopards, bison, ratel, the UK's only herd of breeding elephants, and many endangered species of monkeys. All are housed in natural enclosures with the aim of breeding offspring to be returned to safe wild areas. John Aspinall's other wild animal park is Port Lympne, near Hythe (see page 51).

Open all year, daily. Closed 25 Dec.

BELTRING

HAMLET ON B2015, 2 MILES (3KM) N OF PADDOCK WOOD

A tiny place dominated by the Whitbread Hop Farm, a heritage centre dedicated to the Victorian brewing industry.

Visitors enjoying the sunshine outside the pub in Beltring

The largest group of Victorian oast houses and galleried barns in the world stands at the centre of this stunning complex. Attractions include the Hop Story Exhibition, designed using modern audio-visual technology, the Whitbread Shire Horse Centre, birds of prey including daily owl-flying displays, a rural museum, animal village, pottery workshop, restaurant, play area, nature trail and gift shop. Special events are held during the year. Telephone for details.

Open all year, daily. Closed 25–26 Dec & 31 Dec.

(See also Walk: The Medway at East Peckham, page 34.)

Whitbread Hop Farm
ON A228
Tel: 01622 872068

This attractive village, strung along a ridge with a spacious green, is famous for cricket. The well-known girls' public school lies to the west of the village.

BENENDEN
Village on B2086, 3 miles (5km) SE of Cranbrook

The village has medieval and modern houses separated by bright gardens. Marble from Bethersden was used for the altar stairs at Canterbury Cathedral. The quarries are now worked out.

BETHERSDEN
Village off A28, 6 miles (9.5km) SW of Ashford

A delightful village with bungalows and newer houses set among the older cottages with pretty gardens. There are superb views across the High Weald.

BIDBOROUGH
Village on B2176, 3 miles (5km) SW of Tonbridge

Antique shops, tea shops, pubs and restaurants fill most of Biddenden's half-timbered buildings. The Two Maids of Biddenden on the village sign are Siamese twins said to have been born in the 12th century.

BIDDENDEN
Village on A262, 6 miles (9.5km) NW of Tenterden

The present vineyard was established in 1969 and now covers 22 acres (9ha). Visitors are welcome to stroll around the vineyard and to taste the wines, ciders and apple juice available at the shop. Special events are held during the year.

Open all year, Mar–Dec daily; Jan–Feb most days. Closed Xmas.

Biddenden Vineyards
At Little Whatmans, ½mile (1km) off A262
Tel: 01580 291726

A relatively quiet Thanet resort with cliffs and bays on the north coast, Birchington is the burial place of the Pre-Raphaelite artist and poet, Dante Gabriel Rossetti. Near by stands Quex House, a fine Regency building with lovely period rooms. Adjoining the house is the Powell-Cotton Museum displaying the magnificent African and Oriental collections of the Victorian explorer and anthropologist. Quex Park is dominated by an extraordinary bell tower with a peal of 12 bells.

BIRCHINGTON
Village off A28, 4 miles (6km) W of Margate

This unpretentious little village is compactly grouped beneath the North Downs. All Saints' Church is situated on a hill rising steeply to the north.

BIRLING
Village off A20, 6 miles (9.5km) NW of Maidstone

13

BLEAN
VILLAGE ON A290, 3 MILES (5KM) NW OF CANTERBURY

The village is a scatter of houses on the hills north of Canterbury amid the dwindled remains of the ancient Forest of Blean, the former domain of royal huntsmen and later a haunt of smugglers. Blean Woods, the surviving part of the forest, is a nature reserve managed as coppice with a wide variety of woodland plants and animals.

BOROUGH GREEN
VILLAGE OFF A25, 5 MILES (8KM) E OF SEVENOAKS

The pleasant, large modern village developed around the railway station between the North Downs and the Kentish orchards. The beautiful gardens of Great Comp lie just to the east.

Great Comp
TEL: 01732 882669

Sited in the beautiful wooded countryside of the Weald of Kent, Great Comp gardens surround a 17th-century house. Mr and Mrs Roderick Cameron originally bought an area of 4½ acres (2ha), but land was added in 1962 and 1975 so that today the gardens cover 7½ acres (3ha). Considerable devastation was caused by the great storms of 1987 and 1990, but Great Comp remains a successful combination of a plantsman's garden, with over 3,000 named plants (including no fewer than 30 varieties of magnolia), and one of changing vistas employing curving walks through colourful woodland and focal points such as a group of ruins, a temple and several urns.

Entering on the north side of the garden you come on to a spacious lawn sloping up to a top terrace. Viburnums predominate in the shrub and herbaceous border, and the old yew, *Taxus baccata*, is thought to be more than 150 years old. Two young ginkgoes stand on either side of the steps with a *Photinia x fraseri* close by. The borders here are planted in a cottage-garden style, and although you would expect to find plants like phloxes and violas in such a setting, angel's fishing rods, crocosmias and yuccas are, perhaps, more of a surprise. Several berberis make an attractive impact, as does golden sage, variegated thyme and rue. On the top path the planting of the borders is rich, with colourful azaleas, hydrangeas, Japanese witch hazel and many varieties of magnolia. In the woodland in this eastern part of the garden are a tall silver birch, *Pinus sylvestris* 'Aurea' and a red oak, while beyond a fine American dogwood is a splendid young dawn redwood.

One of the pleasures of Great Comp is the sudden appearance of long views in the depths of beautiful woodland. From the Lion Summerhouse, a tastefully converted privy, there is a splendid view of the garden's 'Place de l'Etoile', embellished with a Doulton urn. In the same area, the 'ruins' were created 15 years ago, and conifers, heathers and rock plants enhance their picturesque effect At the garden's southern boundary a long, straight path joins the Vine urn with the Temple, and from this vantage point you can see both winter

and summer heathers. The shrub planting includes the American smoke bush, and *Pinus coulteri* with its abnormally long needles. Near the Temple, erected in 1973, is a wonderful weeping pear, as well as a Nootka cypress.

Returning to the house a *Magnolia x veitchii* can be seen underplanted with hostas, ferns, irises, lysimachia and polygonum, and in the herbaceous borders in the Square, plume poppies, pink, yellow and white achillea, sedums, euonymus, yuccas and begonias add their seasonal colour.

Garden open daily, Apr–Oct.

The back of Great Comp overlooks an expanse of well kept lawn, deeply cut with beds and borders

BOUGHTON ALUPH
VILLAGE OFF A28, 4 MILES (6.5KM) NE OF ASHFORD

The village, a classic group of a manor house and a church hidden up a no-through road, is home to the Stour Music Festival.

BOUGHTON MALHERBE
HAMLET OFF A20, 2 MILES (3KM) SW OF LENHAM

This little hillside hamlet lies among the orchards above the headwaters of the River Stour and River Beult. There are pleasant views from the village.

BOUGHTON MONCHELSEA
VILLAGE OFF A229, 4 MILES (6.5KM) S OF MAIDSTONE

This is a modern hilltop village with views right over the Weald. The church and lovely Boughton Monchelsea Place perch halfway down steep Quarry Hills. Boughton Monchelsea Place, a splendid battlemented manor house, was built in 1567 and restored in Regency times. It is set in lovely grounds with a deer park.

BOUGHTON STREET
VILLAGE OFF A2, 5 MILES (8KM) W OF CANTERBURY

Boughton Street, an attractive village of Tudor and 18th-century houses lies on Watling Street, the route of the Canterbury pilgrims who first glimpsed the cathedral from the hill beyond.

BOXLEY
VILLAGE OFF A249, 2 MILES (3KM) N OF MAIDSTONE

This pleasant village lies at the foot of the steeply wooded North Downs. The church, associated with notorious Boxley Abbey, retains a chamber for viewing relics.

BRABOURNE
VILLAGE OFF A20, 6 MILES (9.5KM) E OF ASHFORD

The village is a cluster of cottages with a pub and a sturdy church, tucked beneath the steep-faced North Downs in gently rolling country.

BRANDS HATCH
CAR RACING TRACK OFF A20, 3 MILES (5KM) SE OF FARNINGHAM

The world-famous motor-racing circuit hosts the British Grand Prix, other major Formula One races and a variety of other motoring events.

BRASTED
VILLAGE ON A25, 2 MILES (3KM) E OF WESTERHAM

A delightfully rural village of tile-hung cottages on land which rises southwards to the renowned Emmetts Garden on Ide Hill.

Emmetts Garden
IDE HILL. 1M (1.5KM) S OF A25
TEL: 01732 750367

Emmetts (National Trust) is a charming hillside shrub garden, with rare trees, bluebells in spring and fine autumn colours. There are magnificent views over Bough Beech Reservoir and the Weald.
   Open Mar, wknds; Apr–Oct selected afternoons.

BRENZETT
VILLAGE ON A259, 5 MILES (8KM) NW OF NEW ROMNEY

Brenzett is a small settlement on the Rhee Wall, an ancient, probably Roman, sea embankment on wide Romney Marsh. The Peasants' Revolt of 1381 mustered here.

The town, a family seaside resort on the Isle of Thanet between Ramsgate and Margate, grew with the amalgamation of St Peter's, about a mile inland, and Broadstairs and Reading Street on the coast. It retains a village atmosphere. The annual Dickens Festival celebrates the novelist's attachment to the place. The Folk Festival Week in August is one of the leading folk festivals in southern England.

The house was a favourite seaside residence of the novelist Charles Dickens. He wrote the greater part of *David Copperfield* and other works here, and drafted the idea for *Bleak House*. There are special exhibitions of relics salvaged from the Goodwin Sands, and of 'The Golden Age of Smuggling'.
    Open Etr–Nov.

BROADSTAIRS
TOWN ON A255, 2 MILES
(3KM) N OF RAMSGATE

Bleak House Dickens Maritime & Smuggling Museum
FORT RD
TEL: 01843 862224

Bleak House

This house was immortalised by Charles Dickens in *David Copperfield* as the home of the hero's aunt, Betsy Trotwood. Dickens' letters and possessions are shown, with local and Dickensian prints, costumes and general Victoriana. The parlour is furnished as described in the novel.
    Open Apr–mid Oct, daily, afternoons.

Dickens House Museum
VICTORIA PDE
TEL: 01843 862853

BROOK
*VILLAGE OFF A28, 4 MILES
(6.5KM) E OF ASHFORD*

Pleasant houses and cottages and a remarkable Norman church make up this scattered village which lies in wooded farmland beneath the North Downs.

BROOKLAND
*VILLAGE ON A259, 5 MILES
(8KM) W OF NEW ROMNEY*

This attractive village is situated on a little knoll that was once an island in Romney Marsh. The church has an unusual, separate 13th-century bell tower.

CANTERBURY
*CITY OFF A2, 54 MILES (87KM)
SE OF LONDON*

Canterbury is a bustling modern city of venerable age, and a place of pilgrimage for the historically-minded. It was the capital of the Iron Age kingdom of the Cantii – the name survives in today's city and in the county of Kent – and then an important Roman town. In AD 602 St Augustine re-dedicated a deserted Roman church within the city wall, creating Christchurch Cathedral, and Canterbury has been the spiritual capital of England ever since. By c1100 it also had a Norman castle.

*Canterbury Royal Museum is
housed in a fine
timber-framed building*

The cathedral was rebuilt between 1170 and 1175, creating the bulk of the present magnificent Gothic building. The nave was rebuilt again in 1380 and the great central tower went up in 1500. The shrine of Thomas à Becket, murdered here in 1170, was particularly sumptuous. For 200 years it was, Rome apart, the most popular shrine in Europe, thronged by pilgrims, most of whom travelled from London, as did Chaucer's famous group of 1388. The shrine declined in the 15th century and in 1538 it was wrecked by Henry VIII's officers.

Industry flourished when 16th-century Flemish refugees set up a woollen cloth industry, while in the late 17th century Huguenot refugees developed silk weaving. The Weavers' Houses in High Street date from this time, as does St Dunstan's Street.

Devastating bombing in World War II destroyed much of the city's historic heart, but the cathedral survived, as do many timber-framed buildings of the 16th and 17th centuries. Particularly good are Mercery Lane with overhanging buildings and glimpses of the cathedral, and the tiny butter market outside Christchurch Gate of 1517. Post-war clearance has opened up the area around the medieval city walls which run along the Roman lines. Canterbury became a university city in 1962 when the University of Kent was built on a hill to the north.

This award-winning museum is in a breathtaking medieval building on the river bank close to the cathedral, shops and other attractions. The tour starts in Roman times and continues up to the present day. Some of the most exciting of the city's treasures are shown: the Canterbury Cross, Anglo-Saxon gold, and Viking finds. The displays feature (among many others) a reconstruction of Becket's tomb; a medieval street with a pilgrim badge shop; the dramatist Christopher Marlowe (he was born in Canterbury in 1564); the city in the Civil War; and Stephenson's locomotive *Invicta*. The Rupert Bear Gallery and the collection of Joseph Conrad memorabilia are further attractions.

Open all year, daily. Closed Good Fri & Xmas period.

Canterbury Heritage Museum
STOUR ST
TEL: 01227 452747

Underground, at the level of the Roman town, you will find this famous Roman house with its mosaic floors. Following the discoveries of archaeologists, visitors walk through a fascinating reconstruction of Roman buildings, including a market place with stallholders' wares of the period. Displays reveal a wealth of objects rescued by excavations, including 2,000-year-old swords and a silver spoon hoard. A computer-generated reconstruction video guides the tour, and there is a 'touch the past' area where visitors can handle artefacts.

Open all year, most days. Closed Good Fri & Xmas period.

Canterbury Roman Museum
BUTCHERY LN, LONGMARKET
TEL: 01227 785575

Canterbury Royal Museum, Art Gallery & Buffs Regimental Museum
HIGH ST
TEL: 01227 452747

The building houses the city's picture collection including the work of T S Cooper, a leading Victorian animal painter, and the Canterbury and Europe Gallery which displays the fine archaeological objects and decorative arts resulting from close links over the centuries. Regular art events are held in the Special Exhibitions Gallery. The Buffs Regimental Museum tells the story of one of England's oldest infantry regiments.

Open all year, most days. Closed Good Fri and Xmas period.

The Canterbury Tales
SAINT MARGARET'S ST
TEL: 01227 454888

Step back in time to join Chaucer's famous band of pilgrims on their journey to the shrine of St Thomas à Becket in Canterbury Cathedral. Hear their tales of love, greed, chivalry and intrigue and experience life in the 14th century, complete with authentic sights, sounds and smells! Special events are held in the summer, telephone for details.

Open all year, daily.

Canterbury West Gate Museum
SAINT PETER'S ST
TEL: 01227 452747

The last of the city's fortified gatehouses sits astride the London road with the river serving as a moat. Rebuilt in around 1380 by Archbishop Sudbury, it was used as a prison for many years. The battlements give a splendid panoramic view of the city and are a good vantage point for taking photographs. Arms and armour are on display in the guardroom, and the cells in the towers can be visited.

Open all year, most days. Closed Good Fri & Xmas period.

St Augustine's Abbey
LONGPORT (OFF A28)
TEL: 01227 767345

The abbey (English Heritage), founded by St Augustine in AD 598, when he brought Christianity from Rome to England, is one of the oldest monastic sites in the country. It is fascinating to trace the signs of the various phases of the abbey's long history in its ruins.

Open all year, daily. Closed 24–26 Dec & 1 Jan.

This large residential village is perched above the English Channel. The name comes from the little church, originally the outlying chapel of St Radegund's Abbey, Alkham.

The Channel Tunnel, see page 24 and page 38.

The town clusters between a fork in two main roads on the steep slopes of the North Downs; the attractive High Street, with Tudor houses, climbs the steep hill. Charing is a possible site of the Roman town of *Durolenum*, and certainly one of Kent's oldest townships, with a former palace of the Archbishops of Canterbury where both Henry VII and Henry VIII stayed.

The large village, in the valley of the Great Stour beneath wooded downs, clusters around a green with a stately church. It is known for the manufacture of quality paper.

CAPEL LE FERNE
VILLAGE OFF B2011, 3 MILES (5KM) NE OF FOLKESTONE

CHANNEL TUNNEL

CHARING
SMALL TOWN OFF A20, 6 MILES (9.5KM) NW OF ASHFORD

CHARTHAM
VILLAGE OFF A28, 3 MILES (5KM) SW OF CANTERBURY

Tudor houses line the High Street in Charing

CHARTWELL

2 MILES (3KM) S OF
WESTERHAM, OFF B2026
TEL: 01732 866368

In 1924 Winston Churchill and his family moved to Chartwell and it was to remain their happy home for the next 40 years. It is a relatively modest, Victorian house, but it has become one of the most popular of the National Trust's properties – closer, perhaps, to visitors' own aspirations than any great place, and certainly of immense interest as the home of one of our greatest statesmen.

Ceanothus flowers in the gardens of Chartwell

'...I never had a dull or idle moment from morning to midnight, and with my happy family around me dwelt at peace within my habitation.'
Winston Churchill

At Chartwell, Churchill turned his hand to many things, not only the painting and writing for which he is well known, but also the creation, with his own hands, of the garden walls, rockeries and waterworks, and even the large swimming pool. Today the rooms of the house remain very much as they were in Churchill's day, including his studio containing many of his paintings, and his study, in which he did most of his writing.

The Museum and Uniform Rooms contain a selection of his uniforms and many awards and gifts, as well as a 'wanted, dead or alive' poster issued after his escape from a Boer prison in 1899. Elsewhere around the house are reminders of the great man and his interests – old cigar boxes, a painting of his most successful racehorse, the visitors' book recording the great and famous who came to Chartwell between 1924 and 1964, and portraits of family and friends.

Open Apr–Oct, selected afternoons.

This is a busy town on the River Medway with a history of ship-building. It was first used as safer anchorage than Portsmouth by Henry VIII and was developed by Elizabeth I against the Armada, when a large dockyard and arsenal were built. Chatham prospered, but in 1667 the Dutch fleet sailed up the Medway and burnt the English fleet. In response forts were built along the river. The Napoleonic Wars saw further dockyard expansion and Nelson's HMS *Victory* was launched here.

As a child, the novelist Charles Dickens lived in Chatham where his father worked in the Navy Pay Office. Chatham remained England's prime naval dockyard throughout the 19th century, and with the arrival of cement and engineering industries became the largest industrial centre in Kent.

Today, as in the last 400 years, this cheerful, crowded town lives for its dockyards, now an important tourist attraction run as a living museum with flags, sails and rope made in the time-honoured way. There are few old houses, but there is the tiny quadrangle with the chapel and houses of the Sir John Hawkins Hospital, founded in 1592 by the famous navigator 'for poor decayed mariners and shipwrights'.

CHATHAM
*TOWN ON A2, 28 MILES
(45KM) E OF LONDON*

Fort Amherst is the finest Georgian fortress in the country, comprising a large gatehouse, tunnel complex, ditches, magazines, barracks and Civil Defence exhibition. The park-like setting within the fortifications, together with an 1815 re-enactment on most summer Sundays, provides a fascinating visit for all the family.

Open Mar–Oct, daily; Nov–Feb, most days.

Fort Amherst
*DOCK RD
TEL: 01634 847747*

A royal dockyard until 1984, this is now an 80-acre (32-ha) working museum with 47 scheduled ancient monuments which form the most complete Georgian/early Victorian dockyard in the world. Eight museum galleries cover 400 years of ship-building history, and include the RNLI's own museum gallery and the award-winning 'Wooden Walls' which shows through sights, sound and smells, how 18th-century warships such as HMS *Victory* were built here. Visitors can see a working ropery, sail and flag-making, and crafts workshops in action, and witness the restoration of the Victorian sloop *Gannet* in dry dock.

Impressive buildings include huge covered slips, a Georgian Officers' Terrace, and the Commissioner's House (1704) – Britain's oldest intact naval building whose pleasant garden is open to visitors. Horse-drawn wagon rides are available in the summer. Special events are held throughout the year.

Open Etr–early Nov, daily; Feb, Mar & Nov, certain days.

Historic Dockyard
TEL: 01634 812551

CHERITON
VILLAGE OFF M20, ON N OUTSKIRTS OF FOLKESTONE

This former hamlet in a valley above the coast, with a fine 13th-century church, is now a suburb of Folkestone and the site of the Channel Tunnel terminal.

CHIDDINGSTONE
VILLAGE OFF B2027, 4 MILES (6KM) E OF EDENBRIDGE

Arguably the prettiest place in Kent, this picturesque village owned by the National Trust has a lovely street of weather-boarded and tile-hung 16th- and 17th-century houses. The 'Chiding Stone', a block of sandstone, is said to be where nagging wives were scolded.

(See also Cycle ride: Penshurst and Tudor Kent, page 62.)

Chiddingstone Castle
OFF B2027, AT BOUGH BEECH
TEL: 01892 870347

The 'castle' is a 17th-century house, almost completely rebuilt in the castle style c1800 by William Atkinson. It contains Stewart and Jacobite paintings and other relics, Egyptian and Oriental antiquities, and a fine collection of Japanese lacquer and swords. The interior has recently been refurbished with extra rooms open to visitors. The grounds are now undergoing restoration. There is fishing in the lake, for which a fee is payable. Special events are held during the year.

Open Apr–Oct certain days. The castle may be closed at short notice for private functions.

Chiddingstone Castle, reflected in the still waters of its lake

Narrow lanes climb up through Kentish hills and orchards to open out unexpectedly into Chilham's village square, one of Kent's showpieces and often used as a film set. Chilham is used to visitors; for 350 years, after Thomas à Becket's murder, travellers used to pass through on the Pilgrims' Way from Winchester and London to his shrine in Canterbury Cathedral. Today the North Downs Way passes through the town.

Best appreciated out of season, its square is a delightfully haphazard mix of gabled, half-timbered houses, shops and inns dating from the late Middle Ages. Some were refaced in brick in the 18th century. Streets lead down from the corners, each lined with more old houses, some of them overhanging. At either end of the square are the church and the castle. St Mary's stands behind the 15th-century White Horse Inn, built in flint and stone and dominated by its Perpendicular west tower. The castle consists of a Norman keep built on Roman foundations and a Jacobean mansion built by Sir Dudley Digges, a high-ranking official of James I. The lodge gates in the square were added earlier this century, and the grounds laid out by Charles I's gardener, John Tradescant, but reworked by 'Capability' Brown in the 18th century. They house a sanctuary for birds of prey.

CHILHAM
VILLAGE OFF A28, 6 MILES (9.5KM) SW OF CANTERBURY

The village with a small Norman church is in wooded country overlooked by a great white post mill of 1868, restored in 1958.

CHILLENDEN
VILLAGE OFF B2046, 3 MILES (5KM) SE OF WINGHAM

This large village, important in Saxon times, was built on chalk hills at the north-west corner of the Hoo peninsula looking over the Thames marshes and estuary.

CLIFFE
VILLAGE ON B2000, 5 MILES (8KM) N OF ROCHESTER

Laid out in parallel streets on the clifftop above the beach, Cliftonville is the select eastern district of Margate. There is an impressive aquarium on the cliff.

CLIFTONVILLE
AREA OF MARGATE, ON B2051

The historic village lies south of the old Dover road where Tudor almshouses, called Cobham College (1598), incorporate the Hall of Chantry College of 1362. A half-timbered inn, the Leathern Bottle, features in the writing of Dickens, and the church contains notable brasses. Inigo Jones and Robert Adam were involved in the design of magnificent Cobham Hall, now a girls' school.

COBHAM
VILLAGE ON B2009, 4 MILES (6.5KM) SE OF GRAVESEND

This little marshland village on the Hoo peninsula is associated with Dickens' *Great Expectations*. Its massive ruinous castle, 1381, was once owned by Sir John Oldcastle, Shakespeare's Falstaff.

COOLING
VILLAGE OFF B2000, 5 MILES (8KM) NE OF ROCHESTER

25

Walk

A pleasant, easy walk in the Weald of Kent providing good views over the surrounding countryside, and starting from the attractive old town of Cranbrook.

Map ref: TQ776362

INFORMATION

The walk is 4½ miles (7km) long. Fairly level walking, with several stiles and a few steep steps. Can be muddy. One short stretch of road walking. Pubs, cafés in both villages; pub in Sissinghurst welcomes children. Toilets in Cranbrook.

START

Cranbrook lies 17 miles (27km) south of Maidstone on the A229. Free car parking in the Jockey Lane car park, off Carriers Road (off High Street by the White Horse pub).

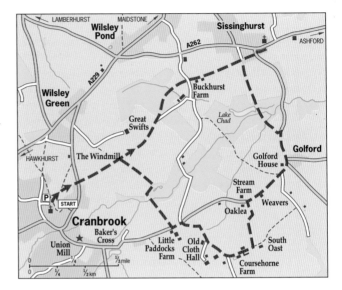

DIRECTIONS

From the top right hand corner of the car park, follow the path left along the churchyard wall. Keep to the hedge at the lower end of a playing field, and go down some steps to a road. Cross over, climb the steps opposite, cross a stile and follow the footpath to meet a concrete track. Continue straight ahead, to cross a stile on the left. Follow the footpath down through woodland, to climb another stile. Cross the field to the stile ahead, and go down the steep steps to cross over a road. Steps opposite lead to a track.

Follow the track until the tracks cross near some houses: keep straight on via Playstole for the village of Sissinghurst.

Return to the crossing of tracks and turn left, to go down by a fence across the fields and into some woods (yellow bands on trees). Pass Lake Chad on your right, following the worn path on the left, and cross over three footbridges by some fallen trees to a stile. Climb this and follow the direction of the yellow marker over a field, to pass through an iron gate to the road. Turn right and walk along the road to Golford crossroads, with Tollgate

Cottage on the left. Turn right here and continue on this narrow road for 800yds (731.5m). Pass by the first footpath sign on the left by 'Weavers' and continue to the footpath sign on the left at 'Oaklea', and follow this through the entrance. Continue ahead to pass through a small gate. Follow the left-hand edge of a playing field, go through a gap in the low railings on to a path, and through another low fence. Turn left and keep to the left of the school playing field to a marked stile, Coursehorne Barn is on your right. Turn right along a wide farm track with duck ponds on your

WHAT TO LOOK OUT FOR

The Union windmill shares your view over the green pastureland of the Weald of Kent on this walk. Look out, too, for the conical roofs of the Kentish oast houses, familiar landmarks in this area.

left, and continue on to a tarmac access road by the entrance to Dulwich College Preparatory School to join a road. Continue past the cemetery on right. Turn left at the T-junction and in a few yards, turn right over a stile. Walk down through a copse to bear right and cross a railed footbridge over a stream. Go straight uphill

and follow around the copse to the right to find a worn path left uphill by a line of hawthorn bushes towards the line of conifer trees. Turn left by gate to return to Cranbrook and the starting point.

Cranbrook

This small Wealden town was once an important centre of the woollen industry. It derived its name from the crane birds which frequented the local stream. There are several fine buildings in the town, but the main attraction is the restored 1814 seven-storey Union Mill.

(See also page 28.)

Sissinghurst

This pretty Wealden village is often overlooked, but well worth exploring. The famous garden and Tudor mansion associated with this name are actually about 1½ miles (2.5km) north-east.

(See also page 79.)

The sturdy windmill at Cranbrook

CRANBROOK

*SMALL TOWN OFF A229,
7 MILES (11KM) W OF
TENTERDEN*

Known as the 'Capital of the Kentish Weald', this delightful little town,
lies among gentle hills near the headwaters of the River Crane. Built
from the profits of the cloth trade, the town has weatherboarded and
brick-and-timber houses and a church with a tall tower. Cranbrook is
dominated by Union Mill, the largest working windmill in England.
(See also Walk: From Cranbrook to Sissinghurst, page 26.)

DARTFORD

*TOWN OFF M25, 12 MILES
(19KM) NW OF ROCHESTER*

*Deal Castle, where Iron Age
weapons and relics of Deal's
history are displayed*

This is an industrial town with a long history, built where Roman
Watling Street crossed the River Darent south of the Thames. There is a
church with Norman foundations and a priory of 1359. A pioneer of
the Industrial Revolution, and important for ship-building, Dartford is the
burial place of Richard Trevithick, the Cornish engineer who worked at
the shipyards. Today the town is known for the Dartford Tunnel and the
Queen Elizabeth II bridge, both carrying traffic across the Thames.

A fishing port and friendly seaside resort, Deal is a delightful jumble of narrow lanes which make dog-legs to divert the driving winds from the Channel. It is a 17th- to 19th-century townscape that, overall, amounts to more than the sum of its individual buildings. These include St Leonard's Church, which is part Norman, but with a cupola maintained by Trinity House as a landmark for shipping; the stately Royal Marine barracks towards Walmer, and three castles built by Henry VIII, namely Deal, Sandown and Walmer. The town is home to the famous Royal Cinque Ports Golf Club.

In 1533 Henry VIII, disappointed at not having produced a healthy son, divorced his Catholic wife, Catherine of Aragon. This move resulted not only in Henry being excommunicated, but also brought him in direct conflict with Catholic France and Spain. In order to protect England's southern coasts, Henry built a series of forts, financed largely from the proceeds of the dissolved monasteries.

Deal and nearby Walmer (both in the care of English Heritage) are two of these forts, both plain, functional buildings, where the sole purpose was defence. At Deal, six semi-circular bastions are joined to form a tower, which is further protected by an outer wall of the same shape. All were liberally supplied with gun loops and cannon ports, so that, in total, an attacker faced five tiers of guns. Walmer has a simpler plan, involving a circular tower and a quatrefoil outer wall, but the defensive principle is the same, and from every angle an invader would face a bristling armoury of handguns and cannon.

As it happened, Henry's precautions were not necessary and Deal was not attacked until 1648, when it was held for Charles I in the Civil War. It suffered extensive damage, but was not attacked again until a bomb fell on it during World War II.

Open all year, most days.

The village is a cheerful handful of timbered cottages away from the main road in wonderfully verdant countryside, with a church hidden among the trees in Denton Park.

The church and vicarage grouped together in a steep lane are the focal point of this village in wooded countryside. Near by are Doddington Place Gardens.

This extensive landscaped garden of 10 acres (4ha) has a spectacular show of springtime colour when the rhododendrons and azaleas are in bloom. There are also formal terraces, fine trees and summer borders.

Open May–Sep, selected afternoons.

DEAL
TOWN OFF A258, 8 MILES (13KM) NE OF DOVER

Deal Castle
VICTORIA ROAD, SW OF DEAL TOWN CENTRE
TEL: 01304 372762

DENTON
VILLAGE ON A260, 7 MILES (11KM) N OF FOLKESTONE

DODDINGTON
VILLAGE OFF A2, 4 MILES (6.5KM) SE OF SITTINGBOURNE

Doddington Place Gardens
TEL: 01795 886101

DOVER

TOWN OFF A2, 15 MILES (24KM) SE OF CANTERBURY

One of England's most important sea ports with exciting docks, Dover owes its existence to its proximity to France – the Eastern Docks are a busy cross-Channel port. The Romans developed Dover as their main naval base and it continued to be important, becoming a founder member of the Confederation of Cinque Ports founded by Edward I. Slowly the old harbour silted up, and it now lies under the town; a new harbour was built out into the English Channel in the 19th century.

Two world wars destroyed much of old Dover – this was Hellfire Corner – and the town itself is a jumble of modernity. Castle Street is the one good street remaining, while the best of the old buildings is Maison Dieu House (1665), now the library.

Dover Castle and Hellfire Corner

TEL: 01304 201628

Dover Castle (English Heritage) is so enormous, and contains so many fascinating features, that it is difficult to know where to start in its description. It was a state-of-the-art castle in medieval times, displaying some of the most highly advanced defensive architecture available. Its strategically vital position at the point where England is nearest to the coast of France has given it a unique place in British history. And it is simultaneously powerful, massive, imposing and splendid.

The castle stands on a spur of rock overlooking the English Channel. The entire site is protected by walls bristling with towers and bulwarks. These include the formidable Constable's Gate, erected in the 1220s, a pair of D-shaped towers that not only served as a serious obstacle for would-be invaders, but provided comfortable lodgings for the castle constables (or, nowadays, their deputies). Outside the walls are earthworks and natural slopes that provide additional defence.

The castle was begun by William the Conqueror, but the great keep was built by Henry II in the 1180s. It is surrounded by yet another wall, studded with square towers and two barbicans. The keep itself is 95ft (29m) tall, and around 95ft (29m) across at its base. There are square turrets at each corner, and even at the top of the tower, where the walls are thinnest, they are still 17ft (5m) thick. The well is carved into the thickness of the wall, and plunges 240ft (73m) to reach a steady water supply.

Dover has had a rich and eventful history, and one especially important episode occurred during the last year of the reign of King John (1216). John's barons had been growing increasingly frustrated with him, and had invited Prince Louis, heir to the French throne, to invade England and take over. Louis landed at Dover and laid siege to Dover Castle, which was held by Hubert de Burgh, a baron loyal to John. Ever since the castle was founded, kings had laid down vast sums of money for its repair and development (notably Henry II and Richard I), and it looked as though this investment had paid off.

Louis, it seemed, would be unable to breach Dover's powerful walls. Then the unthinkable happened – the French managed to take the outer barbican and undermine the gate. Despite de Burgh's efforts, Louis was poised to enter the inner enclosure. With fortunate timing, John died, the barons proclaimed allegiance to his successor, Henry III, and Louis went home. Lessons were learned, however, and Henry spent a good deal of money in improving Dover's defences.

Today much of the castle's 2,000-year history can be experienced by the visitor. The underground tunnel system, nicknamed Hellfire Corner, was originally built in medieval times. Only recently was the veil of official secrecy lifted to reveal that this was the command centre where some of the most important decisions of World War II were made. The visitor can now explore this underground wartime nerve centre and, most recently, share the experience of the soldiers in the hospital and casualty dressing station also hidden here.

Open all year, daily. Closed Xmas.

Visit this beautifully restored working Kentish water mill, enter the Victorian era and discover when traditional country life changed forever and today's technological world was born. Stoneground wholemeal flour is always for sale. Exhibition space now houses the work of local artists and there are short art and craft courses.

Open all year, most days.

Within the grounds of Dover Castle are a Roman lighthouse and a beautiful little Anglo-Saxon church

Crabble Corn Mill
LOWER RD (OFF A2)
TEL: 01304 823292

Old Town Gaol
DOVER TOWN HALL, BIGGIN ST
TEL: 01304 202723

High-tech animation, audio-visual techniques and 'talking heads' take visitors back to Victorian England to experience the horrors of life behind bars, listening, as they walk through the reconstructed courtroom, exercise yard, washroom and cells, to the stories of the felons and their jailers. Visitors can even, if they so wish, try the prisoners' beds or find out what it is like to be locked in a 6ft by 4ft (2m by 1.5m) cell!
Open all year, most days.

Roman Painted House
NEW ST
TEL: 01304 203279

Five rooms of a Roman hotel built 1,800 years ago, now famous for its unique, well-preserved Bacchic frescoes, are open to visitors. The Roman underfloor heating system and part of a late-Roman defensive wall are also on view. There are extensive displays on Roman Dover with videos and commentary. Special events are held throughout the year, telephone for details.
Open Apr–Oct, most days.

The White Cliffs Experience
MARKET SQ
TEL: 01304 214566 & 210101

Beach fishing at Dungeness

This award-winning attraction uses stunning stage effects and the latest in audio-visual techniques to tell the story of Britain through the eyes of Dover from Roman times through to World War II. Visitors will witness a Roman invasion, step aboard on old ferry deck, see the fantastic 'Time and Tide' show and pick their way through the rubble of a 1940s Dover street after its bombardment by enemy shells. There is an

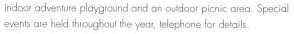

indoor adventure playground and an outdoor picnic area. Special events are held throughout the year, telephone for details.

Open all year, daily. Closed 25 & 26 Dec.

This glorious shingle foreland, with an expanse of marshland and a wild, remote nature reserve with a lighthouse, is on Kent's southerly tip. It is brooded over by nuclear power stations.

The 'A' and 'B' power stations at Dungeness make an extraordinary sight in a landscape of shingle, fishing boats and owner-built houses. There is a high-tech information centre, with 'hands-on' interactive videos and many other displays and models including an environmental exhibition which depicts Dungeness from the Ice Age through to today. The nature trail clearly shows the rare shingle ridges, flora and fauna and completes an interesting day out. Prior bookings for tours is advisable.

Open: Information centre open all year. Regular tours of 'A' & 'B' power stations available. Children under 5 are not allowed on the tours.

A seaside resort with chalets, holiday camps and funfairs, enjoying a sandy beach and the diminutive Romney, Hythe and Dymchurch Railway. Dymchurch is the ancient 'capital of Romney Marsh', on the edge of reclaimed levels 7½ft (2m) below high tide, and protected from the sea by the Dymchurch Wall. The Lords of the Level, administrators of Romney Marsh, still meet at New Hall.

This is one of the many artillery towers (English Heritage) which formed part of a chain of strongholds intended to resist an invasion by Napoleon. It is fully restored, with an original gun on the roof.

Open Etr wknd; May–Jul, wknds only; Aug, daily.

The village lies on the River Medway among hop gardens and orchards, with a superb medieval stone bridge, some old cottages, bungalows, caravan parks and boatyards.

There are old buildings in the village centre with pleasant Kentish cottages by the church, and a modern development in the old park of Clare House. The village is famed for its horticultural research station.

This is a large village with several outlying hamlets set in beautiful countryside deep among the hop gardens.

(See also Walk: The Medway at East Peckham, page 34.)

DUNGENESS
HEADLAND OFF B2075, 5 MILES (8KM) SE OF LYDD

Dungeness Visitor Centre
TEL: 01797 321815

DYMCHURCH
SMALL TOWN ON A259, 5 MILES (8KM) SW OF HYTHE

Martello Tower
ACCESS FROM HIGH ST, NOT FROM SEAFRONT

EAST FARLEIGH
VILLAGE ON B2010, 2 MILES (3KM) SE OF MAIDSTONE

EAST MALLING
VILLAGE OFF A20, 4 MILES (6.5KM) W OF MAIDSTONE

EAST PECKHAM
VILLAGE OFF B2016, 4 MILES (6.5KM) NE OF TONBRIDGE

This is a short, pleasant waterside walk that is packed with attractions, including a canal lock, a nature reserve, an island and a unique view of oast houses.

Map ref: TQ487667

INFORMATION

The walk is around 2½ miles (4km) long.

Level, easy ground.

Several stiles.

Pubs in East Peckham: The Merryboys does not allow children inside but there is a garden; bar meals and morning coffee served; The Queen Tavern allows children in at Sunday lunch time and has a garden.

Grassy area at lock suitable for picnics.

START

East Peckham is 4 miles (6.5km) east of Tonbridge, off the A26. Start the walk from The Merryboys pub in the village centre. There is a car park in the road opposite the pub and behind the Methodist church.

DIRECTIONS

Walk south past the fish and chip shop to the next crossroads by the Queen Tavern. Turn right to follow a farm track leading to a footbridge. Bear half right to reach Sluice Weir Lock on the River Medway. Cross the lock gates and go left to walk over the weir stream on the high concrete bridge.

Turn right along a woodland footpath which follows a fence. At a stile the path enters the Beltring Hop Farm nature reserve. After a footbridge, the path passes between a lake and a stream before entering a large field. Turn half right to walk parallel to the stream to find a three-arm signpost by a footbridge. Cross the stream

In Beltring Hop Farm's nature reserve

and turn immediately right across a second bridge. Follow the path ahead, which turns left past a wood to a point near the far corner of the field. A wooden waymark post indicates the approach to a bridge flanked by stiles leading on to Bullen Island in the Medway. Keep to the right on the island to cross the next bridge, which spans the main navigation channel.

On the mainland the path follows the River Bourne to a stile. Turn left over a footbridge and go immediately right to follow the Bourne upstream. Cross the water again on reaching another footbridge by Millstream Cottages. Turn right on to a footpath which follows a fence. After a double bend the path, known as the King's Highway, widens to run below two banks. Cross a stile to enter Snoll Hatch and turn right to follow the main street past the former post office and around the corner. A pavement follows the road into the centre of East Peckham.

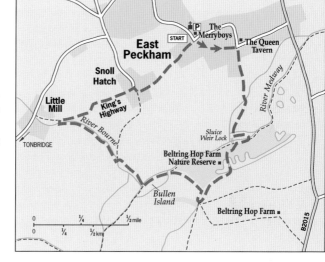

East Peckham

There is no old church in this village because the community has drifted south to the river, leaving its 14th-century church isolated 2 miles (3km) away. On its present site the village has three pubs surviving from the days when hop pickers from London thronged the area every autumn. (See also page 33.)

Whitbread Hop Farm

The hop farm, where hops were handpicked until as recently as 1969, has the largest group of Victorian oast houses and galleried barns in the world, now housing two award-winning museums. Of the many events and attractions here, the greatest must be the magnificent shire horses that pull the Lord Mayor of London's golden coach, making the two hour journey to the City each November in their specially built horse box.

(See also page 12.)

King's Highway

The east–west footpath linking Little Mill with Snoll Hatch was part of the original Tonbridge-to-Maidstone main road until replaced by a 'new' road in 1763.

Common rockrose

WHAT TO LOOK OUT FOR

Kingfishers frequent the River Medway and cuckoos can be heard in spring. On Bullen Island purple loosestrife, thistles and cow parsley grow among the many meadow plants. Along the River Bourne, several species of dragonfly can be found resting among the reeds.

EASTCHURCH

VILLAGE ON B2231, 2 MILES (3KM) SE OF MINSTER

Eastchurch is an agricultural village, developed but pleasing, built among trees in the middle of the Isle of Sheppey, on the island's only east–west road. Eastchurch Aerodrome was Britain's first airfield (1909); both Lord Brabazon and Sir Winston Churchill learnt to fly here. Later it was important during the Battle of Britain.

EASTRY

VILLAGE ON A256, 3 MILES (5KM) SW OF SANDWICH

This village with its many historical connections was built along the straight Roman road from Richborough to Dover. Eastry Court stands on the site of a palace of Saxon Kentish kings, where Thomas à Becket hid in 1164 on his flight to France. Lord Nelson stayed at Heronden House, and one of his officers, Captain John Harvey, is buried here.

EBBSFLEET

SITE ON A256, IMMEDIATELY SW OF CLIFFS END

Ebbsfleet, dominated by its power station on a great meandering loop near the mouth of River Stour, was the landing place of Hengist and Horsa in AD 499 and St Augustine in AD 597.

Colourful window boxes adorn the brick-and-timbered buildings in Elham

ELHAM

VILLAGE OFF A260, 6 MILES (9.5KM) NW OF FOLKESTONE

The village is set in the pastoral Elham Valley above the River Little Stour – a 'nailbourne' or intermittent stream. Elham was once a market town, its charter granted by Edward I, and the delightful market square at the centre is surrounded by brick-and-timbered houses and brick-and-tile cottages with new buildings that harmonise pleasingly.

EYNSFORD

VILLAGE ON A225, 5 MILES (8KM) S OF DARTFORD

A picturesque and popular village beside a narrow hump-backed bridge and ancient ford in the Darent Valley. Here the picture-postcard Plough Inn, old timbered cottages and a slim-spired church group themselves beside the ruined 11th-century castle. The rest of the village is strung along the main road.

(See also: A Walk to Lullingstone Castle, page 48.)

The walls of this castle (English Heritage), still 30ft (9m) high, come as a surprise in the pretty little village. The castle was begun in the 11th century by William de Eynsford, who later retired to become a monk. Also to be seen are the remains of the castle hall and ditch.

Open all year, any reasonable time.

Eynsford Castle
(OFF A225)
TEL: 01322 862536

Lower Eythorne is an attractive Kentish village of pretty cottages and a church with rare lead font. There are newer houses in Upper Eythorne, an old colliery village.

EYTHORNE, UPPER AND LOWER
VILLAGES OFF A256, 5 MILES
(8KM) N OF DOVER

This is an attractive village on the River Darent, close to the M20, with good 18th-century houses and a church in a grove of yew trees.

FARNINGHAM
VILLAGE OFF A225, 5 MILES
(8KM) S OF DARTFORD

A superb small town amid orchards at the head of a creek, Faversham was attached to the Cinque Port of Dover from 1225 and still possesses a commercial quay. Long associated with gunpowder mills, bricks and brewing, the town is now a centre for packaging and the distribution of fruit, and is still the brewing capital of Kent.

Faversham was granted its first charter in AD 811, and the town centres on Market Square, where a market is still held. Abbey Street is the show street, restored since 1961 as part of a conservation scheme. It is named after the abbey founded by King Stephen in 1147 and destroyed at the Reformation. The houses in Abbey Street are mellowed brick and half-timbered, leading to 17th-century warehouses on Standard Quay, built with reused stone and timbers from the abbey. Number 80 is part of the abbey gatehouse, rebuilt in 1538–40 for Thomas Arden, mayor. He was murdered here in 1550 and his tale is told in *Arden of Faversham*, a play of 1592.

West Street is another rewarding street of half-timbered buildings. The church has a graceful 'flying spire', a well-loved landmark.

FAVERSHAM
TOWN OFF M2, 8 MILES
(13KM) SE OF SITTINGBOURNE

A thousand years of history and architecture in Faversham are shown in award-winning displays, an audio-visual programme, and a working vintage telephone exchange in this 16th-century building (a former coaching inn). There is a Tourist Information Centre and a bookshop. A special event held every year is the Faversham Open House Scheme when over 20 historic properties in Faversham, usually not open to the public, can be visited on certain dates. Admission to the properties is by programme only; for more details contact the Fleur de Lis Heritage Centre.

Open all year, Apr–Sep, daily; Oct–Etr, most days.

Fleur de Lis Heritage Centre
13 PRESTON ST
TEL: 01795 534542

FOLKESTONE
TOWN OFF M20, 14 MILES (22.5KM) E OF ASHFORD

The landfall point of the Channel Tunnel and the great mass of overhead power cables for the trains have transformed the coastal scenery at Folkestone, a channel port since Saxon times from which the French coast is visible on clear days.

Two world wars have battered both the old town, with steep narrow steps leading down to the fishing harbour and ferry terminal, and the expansive Victorian resort, developed after the railway arrived in 1842. Yet the old town preserves the Georgian streets (the cobbled High Street is pedestrianised), and the sedate Victorian developments of the 1860s and 70s retain their charm, including the glorious clifftop promenade called the Leas, backed by stuccoed houses. A lift of 1885, powered by water pressure, takes visitors down to the Maritime Gardens and Undercliff Road. The old fish market, The Stade, at the bottom of the High Street, was rebuilt in the 1930s, and leads to East Cliff Sands. The beach is much frequented by wind-surfers.

Near by is Folkestone Warren, formed by a coastal landslide in 1915, and dubbed 'Little Switzerland'. It is known for its rare wild flowers.

Linking Britain to the Continent physically for the first time since the English Channel was formed some 9,500 years ago, the Channel Tunnel – actually three tunnels – is one of the 20th century's most exciting engineering achievements. The idea was far from new, and had been suggested in France well over a hundred years ago. A French engineer presented Napoleon Bonaparte with a plan for a tunnel to accommodate horse-drawn carriages, but the English had reason to distrust

The crazy golf course is well situated on the seafront at Folkestone

Napoleon's motives. Work on a tunnel eventually began from both ends in 1877, but was halted after an outcry in England. Digging the present tunnel began in 1986, and the French and English tunnelling parties met and joined hands beneath the Channel on 1 December 1990. On that day Britain ceased to be an island.

In the 18th century Folkestone was noted for its fishing fleet; today it is best known as a Channel port. The museum has displays on its history up to World War II and also has fossils, natural history and archaeology exhibits. The gallery houses changing exhibitions of work by local and national artists and major exhibitions on local themes – a programme of events is published. Music and drama events are occasionally held.

Open all year, most days.

Museum & Art Gallery
2 Grace Hill
Tel: 01303 850123

FORDWICH
VILLAGE OFF A28, 2 MILES (3KM) NE OF CANTERBURY

This pleasant village, by a bridge on the River Stour, has a splendid group of buildings around the church and what is beleived to be the smallest town hall in England.

Town Hall
THE SQUARE (OFF A28)
TEL: 01227 710756

The timber-framed Tudor town hall and courtroom is thought to be the oldest and smallest in England. It overlooks the River Stour, peaceful now but hectic in the Middle Ages, because Fordwich was the port for Canterbury. The old town jail can also be visited.
Open Etr & Jun–Sep, afternoons.

GILLINGHAM
TOWN ON A2, IMMEDIATELY E OF CHATHAM

A lively town on the Thames estuary, adjoining Chatham, with a variety of sporting facilities, and a country park overlooking the internationally important waterfowl reserves on North Kent Marshes.

Royal Engineers Museum
PRINCE ARTHUR RD, BROMPTON (OFF B2004)
TEL: 01634 406397

The museum is a treasure trove of the unexpected, covering the world-wide work of the Royal Engineers from 1066. Learn about the first military divers, photographers, aviators and surveyors; see exhibits as diverse as 24 Victoria Crosses, the regalia of four Field Marshals, memorabilia relating to General Gordon and Field Marshal Lord Kitchener, Wellington's battle map from Waterloo and a Harrier jump-jet.
Open all year, most days. Closed Good Fri, 25–26 Dec & 1 Jan.

GOODNESTONE
VILLAGE OFF B26046, 2 MILES (3KM) S OF WINGHAM

The village lies in the great park of Goodnestone House, with gardens, including a walled garden, woodland garden and arboretum, open to the public.

GOUDHURST
VILLAGE ON A262, 4 MILES (6KM) NW OF CRANBROOK

A popular and picturesque hilltop village in the High Weald, set among the orchards and hopfields. The High Street has attractive tile-hung, weatherboarded and timbered houses and a village pond replete with ducks of several kinds, including muscovies. Smuggling was rife here in the 18th century and the Star and the Eagle pub is said to have a secret passage connecting it to the 14th-century church. The stocky church tower, which dates from 1638 when a violent storm damaged the original, was used a look-out post in both world wars.

Finchcocks
OFF A262
TEL: 01580 211702

This fine early Georgian house stands in a spacious park with a beautiful garden, and contains an outstanding collection of keyboard instruments dating from the 17th century onwards. They have been restored to playing condition, and there are musical tours on all open days and private visits. Visually handicapped visitors may touch the instruments as well as hear them.
Open Etr–Oct, some afternoons.

gazetteer

Village houses overlook the duck pond in Goudhurst

This is the northern tip of the flat and windswept Hoo peninsula at the confluence of the Thames and Medway estuaries. The seaside village of Grain is noted for its oil refinery.

Gravesend is a busy, noisy, bustling town by the River Thames, where it narrows to become 'London River', and coastal pilots hand over control of their ships to river pilots. It has a long seafaring history and fleets were assembled here in Elizabethan times. Today, sailing clubs keep up the tradition; the town also has a museum, leisure centre and an old-fashioned daily market.

The village, on the Kent/Sussex border, is associated with a big house, Groombridge Place. The Kent (northern) part of the village consists of attractive tile-hung cottages of the Groombridge estate grouped around a triangular green with a brick church (1625), originally a private chapel. Groombridge Place gardens feature walled gardens laid out in the 17th century against the backdrop of a moated house. The Enchanted Forest, with pools and waterfalls, overlooks the Weald.

GRAIN, ISLE OF
ISLAND ON A228, OFF N COAST OF KENT

GRAVESEND
TOWN ON A226, 7 MILES (11KM) NW OF ROCHESTER

GROOMBRIDGE
VILLAGE ON B2110, 4 MILES (6.5KM) SW OF TUNBRIDGE WELLS

HAMSTREET
VILLAGE ON A2070, 6 MILES (9.5KM) S OF ASHFORD

The village is situated above the former cliff-line behind Romney Marsh. There are a few old houses at the centre, and it is backed by pleasant Ham Street Woods, threaded with paths.

HARBLEDOWN
SUBURB OFF A2, IMMEDIATELY W OF CANTERBURY

This old village was traditionally the last halt of pilgrims on their way to Canterbury; the classic view to the cathedral vanished in the expansion of the city that has engulfed Harbledown.

HARRIETSHAM
VILLAGE ON A20, 7 MILES (11KM) SE OF MAIDSTONE

Harrietsham is a pleasant village severed by the A20, with a church on a hill to the north. East Street, with attractive tiled and weatherboarded houses, is beside a lake to the south.

HARTY, ISLE OF
ISLAND OFF B2231, PART OF THE ISLE OF SHEPPEY

This is the remote, windswept south-eastern tip of the Isle of Sheppey, overlooking the estuarine mud of the Swale. It is inhabited by flocks of waders and visited by many migrating birds.

HAWKHURST
VILLAGE ON A268/A229, 4 MILES (6.5KM) S OF CRANBROOK

At the heart of this large straggling Wealden village, the church and weatherboarded cottages are set around a big tree-lined green. The newer centre at the crossroads has an elegant Regency shopping arcade.

HAWKINGE
VILLAGE OFF A260, 3 MILES (5KM) N OF FOLKESTONE

Set high on the chalk above Folkestone, the village is home to the Battle of Britain Museum and a humble little flint church which was declared redundant in 1980.

Kent Battle of Britain Museum
AERODROME RD, ON A260
TEL: 01303 893140

A former Battle of Britain Station, the aerodrome houses the largest collection of authentic relics and related memorabilia of British and German aircraft involved in the fighting. Also shown are British and German uniforms and equipment, and full-size replicas of the Hurricane, Spitfire and ME 109 used in Battle of Britain films.
Open Etr–Oct, daily.

HEADCORN
VILLAGE ON A274, 9 MILES (14.5KM) SE OF MAIDSTONE

A large, attractive village beside the River Beult, now in commuter-land, Headcorn has excellent half-timbered houses from its days as a prosperous cloth-making town.

HERNE BAY
TOWN ON A299, 7 MILES (11KM) N OF CANTERBURY

A popular resort on the north Kent coast, Herne Bay has a 7-mile (11-km) beach and a seafront dominated by an 80-ft (243-m) clock tower of 1837. The town has sailing clubs, a golf course, and a country park and there is a leisure centre on the seafront, where the former pier (burned down in 1970) once stood. The local museum, a windmill of 1789 and a church are inland at the old centre of Herne.

The 19th-century clock tower is a familiar landmark on the seafront at Herne Bay

The 20-acre (8-ha) park has a nature trail leading through woodland where many birds and animals including fallow and sika deer, mara, guanaco, wallaby, owls, Scottish wildcats and red foxes may be seen. Small rare-breed farm animals, ponies and a miniature donkey may be fed with the food sold at the gate. There are also a walk-in rabbit enclosure and an indoor garden, an adventure playground and an under-fives' playground.

Open Etr–Dec, daily.

The village is high on wooded hills above Faversham with splendid views over Graveney Marshes and Mount Ephraim Gardens. The church is set beside a pretty green with an oak tree and characterful buildings.

HERNE COMMON
'Brambles' Wildlife Park
AT WEALDON FOREST PK
ON A291, 3 MILES (5KM) S OF
HERNE BAY
TEL: 01227 712379

HERNHILL
VILLAGE OFF A299, 3 MILES
(5KM) E OF FAVERSHAM

HEVER
VILLAGE OFF B2026, 2 MILES (3KM) SE OF EDENBRIDGE

Hever Castle
TEL: 01732 865224

Romantic Hever Castle, once the home of Anne Boleyn.

The village is famous for its moated castle where Henry VIII wooed Anne Boleyn. The church at the gates has Bullen (Boleyn) tombs.

(See also Cycle ride: Penshurst and Tudor Kent, page 62.)

Romance, intrigue, wealth, power and far-reaching decisions – all have been played out on the stage of Hever Castle. This was the childhood home of Anne Boleyn, for whom Henry VIII abandoned his wife, his faith and the faith of the nation. Anne's fate is well known, and her parents died, broken, within two years. Henry later gave Hever to his divorced wife, Anne of Cleves. Over the centuries Hever went into a decline until, in 1903, it was bought by William Waldorf Astor who spent substantial amounts of his $100 million fortune on restoring the castle to its former magnificence. The castle proved too small for the Astors' lavish entertaining and the inspired solution was to build the 'Tudor Village'. This picturesque cluster of apparently individual cottages actually consists of 100 luxurious rooms, linked by corridors and a covered bridge over the moat to the castle.

Today Hever is as much a monument to early 20th-century craftsmanship as it is to the past. Room after room of splendid panelling and intricate carving blend perfectly with the original timbers. The rooms are furnished with antiques; walls are hung with splendid tapestries, one depicting Princess Mary's marriage to Louis XII

of France, with Anne Boleyn reputedly among the attendants; portraits include a Holbein of Henry VIII, and Queen Elizabeth I by John Bettes the Younger. The dark and oppressive Henry VIII Room, with its great four-poster bed, is evocative of the period, but the most poignant is Anne Boleyn's Room, containing the prayer book she took with her to her execution.

Open Mar–Nov, afternoons.

A scattered village on the edge of the Thames–Medway conurbation, with an ancient marshland church, Higham incorporates three separate hamlets, the most southerly being Glads Hill, where Dickens lived from 1857 to 1870.

HIGHAM
VILLAGE OFF A226, 3 MILES (5KM) NW OF ROCHESTER

Centred on its pleasant green, this big and busy village in the heart of the Kentish hopfields and orchards has agreeable weatherboarded and half-timbered buildings.

HORSMONDEN
VILLAGE ON B2162, 3 MILES (5KM) NE OF LAMBERHURST

This small village lies on the edge of parkland near Godinton Park, a rambling red-brick house of 1628 with a garden laid out in formal style in the 18th century and topiary hedges of the 20th century. Nearby Hothfield Common nature reserve covers 140 acres (57ha). It is mostly gorse and bracken with bog asphodel in waterlogged places, and rare plants and animals.

HOTHFIELD
VILLAGE OFF A20, 3 MILES (5KM) NW OF ASHFORD

Hythe is a seaside place near Romney Marsh, formerly an important member of the Confederation of Cinque Ports. Today it is the terminus of the Romney, Hythe & Dymchurch Railway (see page 56). The Royal Military Canal, built against the Napoleonic threat, divides the seaside resort from the old town, where narrow alleyways and little streets climb up to the big old church.

HYTHE
TOWN ON A259, 4 MILES (6.5KM) W OF FOLKESTONE

A straggling village on the River Little Stour, Ickham has a big, plain 14th-century church and the Old Rectory, a manor house of 1280 with a hall on the first floor.

ICKHAM
VILLAGE OFF A257, 5 MILES (8KM) E OF CANTERBURY

The village consists of a cluster of cottages and a pub around the green in a wonderful position on greensand hills. The National Trust owns about 400 acres (162ha) of woodland and heath with fine viewpoints.

IDE HILL
VILLAGE OFF B2042, 4 MILES (6.5KM) SW OF SEVENOAKS

An attractive old village with pretty, half-timbered cottages and houses. Near by is Oldbury Hill, with palaeolithic rock shelters and an Iron Age fort.

IGHTHAM
VILLAGE OFF A25, 4 MILES (6.5KM) E OF SEVENOAKS

Ightham Mote
2½ MILES (4KM) S OFF A227
TEL: 01732 810378

This beautiful medieval manor house, complete with moat and attractive garden, was given to the National Trust in 1985. It has been extensively remodelled through the centuries but it is still a splendid example of medieval architecture: particularly the Great Hall, Old Chapel and crypt of c1340. The house also contains many important additions from great periods and notable features include the drawing room with its Jacobean fireplace and frieze, its Palladian window and the hand-painted Chinese wallpaper.
     Open end Mar—Oct, most days.

KEMSING
VILLAGE OFF A225, 3 MILES
(5KM) NE OF SEVENOAKS

A pretty village beneath the North Downs, increasingly hemmed in by the overspill from Sevenoaks. There are tile-hung houses around the green and St Edith's Well, whose water is said to cure eye troubles.

KILNDOWN
VILLAGE OFF A262, 2 MILES
(3KM) SW OF GOUDHURST

A tiny place with a colourful Gothic Revival church built in 1839—40, dramatic with stained glass made in Munich, some of which was destroyed during World War II.

LAMBERHURST
VILLAGE ON A21, 6 MILES
(10KM) SE OF TUNBRIDGE
WELLS

This attractive village, which lies in a deep valley on the Kent/Sussex border, was important in the days of the Wealden iron industry, when the village made the railings for St Paul's Cathedral. A sample is displayed in the High Street. The vineyard, started in 1972, is associated with the revival of English wine.

Bayham Abbey
OFF B2169, 2 MILES (3KM)
W IN EAST SUSSEX
TEL: 01892 890381

Set in the wooded Teise valley, these ruins (English Heritage) include parts of the old church, cloisters and gatehouse.
     Open Apr—Sep, daily.
     (See also Cycle ride: Bewl Water and the High Weald, page 8.)

Owl House Gardens
1 MILE (1.5KM) NE OFF A21
TEL: 01892 890230

The Owl House is a small, timber-framed 16th-century house, a former haunt of wool smugglers. Surrounding it are 13 acres (5ha) of gardens with spring flowers, azaleas, rhododendrons, roses, shrubs and ornamental fruit trees. The sweeping lawns lead to lovely woodlands of oak and birch, and sunken water gardens.
     Open all year, daily. Closed 25—26 Dec & 1 Jan.

Scotney Castle Garden
1 MILE (1.5KM) S, ON A21
TEL: 01892 891081

The beautiful gardens at Scotney were carefully planned in the 19th century around the remains of the old, moated Scotney Castle (National Trust). Spring flowers are followed by gorgeous rhododendrons, azaleas and a mass of roses, and then superb autumn colours.
     Open: Garden Etr—Oct; Old Castle May—mid-Sep, most days.
     (See also Cycle ride: Bewl Water and the High Weald, page 8.)

Leigh, pronounced 'Lie', is a pleasant village built around a green. There is a large Victorian Tudor-style house and a restored 13th-century church.

This former market town, still tightly clustered about a pleasant market square, has the church on one side and half-timbered and 18th-century houses on the other three.

West of Maidstone, and within earshot of the M20, the village is a blend of old and new, with part of a 14th-century castle incorporated into a modern house.

Set on a steep hill overlooking the Weald, this peasant and unpretentious village has pairs of ragstone cottages, a Victorian church and a big house of the 1730s set in parkland.

This village is situated on the Kent/Sussex boundary beside the River Teise. Bayham Old Abbey ruins, among the most picturesque monastic remains of southern Britain, are on the Sussex side of the river.

A seaside place on the east side of Dungeness, the village was first laid out in 1886 as a coastal resort planned 'so as in time to form a marine town'.

This little village lies amid orchards facing a creek on the River Medway. The ancient Church of St Margaret of Antioch is separated from the estuary by a dyke.

LEIGH
VILLAGE ON B2027, 3 MILES (5KM) W OF TONBRIDGE

LENHAM
SMALL TOWN OFF A20, 4 MILES (6.5KM) NW OF CHARING

LEYBOURNE
VILLAGE ON A20, 5 MILES (8KM) W OF MAIDSTONE

LINTON
VILLAGE ON A229, 4 MILES (6.5KM) S OF MAIDSTONE

LITTLE BAYHAM
HAMLET OFF B2169, 3 MILES (5KM) W OF LAMBERHURST

LITTLESTONE-ON-SEA
VILLAGE ON B2071, 1 MILE (1.5KM) E OF NEW ROMNEY

LOWER HALSTOW
OFF A2, 4 MILES (6.5KM) NW OF SITTINGBOURNE

*A*rtist Samuel Palmer called this area 'the veil of heaven', and historian Arthur Mee described the view down the Darent Valley as 'unique on the map of rural England'.

Map ref: TQ650546

INFORMATION

The walk is just over 2 miles (3km) long.
Several stiles.
One unmanned level-crossing.
The Plough at Eynsford serves special children's meals in the restaurant; children are also welcome in the bar, and there is a patio.
Tea shop in post office.
Café and picnic tables at the visitor centre.

START

Eynsford is 5 miles (8km) south of Dartford on the A225. Start the walk from the ford, just off the main road, opposite the church. There is a car park at the side of The Plough public house.

DIRECTIONS

From the ford walk past The Plough and Sparepenny Lane, with Home Farm on the left. After the road bends, bear half-right up a slope and go through a gap by a gate. Follow the footpath which rises half-right up the sloping field to cross the railway line. The path continues in the same direction to a stile near the end of a row of trees marking the line of a metalled farm drive.

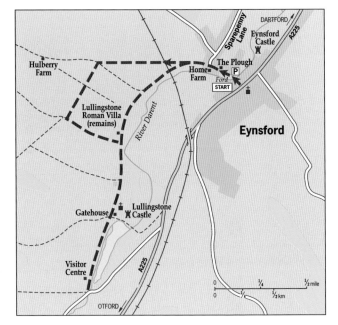

Cross over to a second stile and continue half-right to a stile by a grass farm track. Cross the stile opposite, which is slightly higher up, and keep by the fence on the left.

At the far end of the field cross another stile and turn left on to a narrow path which runs down the hill. In the wood there is a stile, then some steps before meeting a metalled lane. Turn right to visit Lullingstone Castle. Beyond the castle gateway a 700yd (640m) riverside footpath leads to a visitor centre. Retrace your steps back to

Lullingstone Roman Villa and follow the lane, waymarked with a 'D' for the Darent Valley Path, passing under the railway viaduct to return to Eynsford.

Eynsford

The partly Norman church figured in the dispute between Henry II and Thomas à Becket when the archbishop appointed a new priest against the wishes of Sir William de Eynsford. His ruined castle (English Heritage), which incorporates Roman materials, can be visited. John Wesley used

Walk

the narrow 16th-century bridge by the ford as an open-air pulpit. (See also page 36.)

Lullingstone

Lullingstone Castle, with its fine state rooms and beautiful grounds, is well worth a visit. Catherine of Aragon's pomegranate symbol can be found carved on the rood screen inside the little St Botolph's Church, known as 'the church on the lawn'. Visitors may go through the arch and over the lawn to visit the church even when the castle is closed. It was on this grass that the rules of lawn tennis were devised in 1873.

WHAT TO LOOK OUT FOR

Home Farm breeds Highland cattle, which until recently were rarely seen outside Scotland, and from the top of the hill there may be the odd sighting of deer. Among the creatures along the river are water voles and damselflies. Birds include swans, kingfishers and herons.

The Roman villa dates from the first and second centuries. It has an extensive bath complex and well preserved mosaic floors. The site is roofed for protection, with additional exhibits in a gallery. (See also page 50.)

Eynsford from Hulberry Farm

Short-tailed field vole

LULLINGSTONE

Site off A225, 1 mile (1.5km) SW of Eynsford

A church, 18th-century castle and Roman villa can be found in the 600-acre (243-ha) park by the River Darent, where it passes through the North Downs. The small flint-built church displays some very grand monuments while the Roman villa, occupied from the 1st to the 5th centuries, incorporates a Christian chapel, unique in Britain. There are waymarked walks in the park and information and displays at the visitor centre.

Lullingstone Castle

(See also: A Walk to Lullingstone Castle, page 48.)

Lullingstone Castle

1 mile (1.5km) SW of A225
Tel: 01322 862114

The house was altered extensively in Queen Anne's time, and has fine state rooms and beautiful grounds. The 15th-century gate tower was one of the first gatehouses in England to be built entirely of bricks.
Open: house Apr–Sep, wknds.

Lullingstone Roman Villa

(half mile SW off A225)
Tel: 01322 863467

The excavation of this Roman villa (English Heritage) in 1949 uncovered one of the most exciting archaeological finds of the century. Here visitors can see some of the most remarkable villa remains in Britain, including wonderful mosaic tiled floors and wall paintings and the ruins of one of the earliest Christian chapels in Britain.
Open all year, daily. Closed 24–26 Dec & 1 Jan.

LYDD

Town on B2075, 3 miles (5km) SW of New Romney

A large village on Romney Marsh, and once an important port, Lydd was stranded some 3 miles (5km) inland by coastal silting and the great storm of 1287. It has a grand 13th-century church, known as the 'cathedral of Romney Marsh'; the High Street curves gently to it, an attractive mixture of stucco and brick.

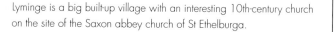
Gazetteer

Lyminge is a big built-up village with an interesting 10th-century church on the site of the Saxon abbey church of St Ethelburga.

The village, with modern housing and Port Lympne Zoo, is set on the old cliff-line above Romney Marsh. The Royal Military Canal is at the base of the cliff. On the cliff is tumble-down Stutfall Castle, the Roman Saxon shore fort *Portus Lemanis* built in AD 270. Shepway Cross is a 1923 replacement of a medieval cross, marking the site of the Court of Shepway, which met to administer the affairs of the Cinque Ports.

This small medieval castle was restored in 1905 and retains much of its former character. The view from the castle includes the Royal Military Canal (dug as part of the coastal defences during the Napoleonic Wars), Romney Marsh and, in fine weather, the French coast across the Channel. There are exhibitions of toys and dolls, reproduction medieval brasses and scale models of English cathedrals.
    Open late May–early Sep, certain days.

John Aspinall's 300-acre (121-ha) wild animal park houses hundreds of rare animals: Indian elephants, wolves, bison, black and snow leopards, Siberian tigers, gorillas and monkeys. The mansion, designed by Sir Herbert Baker, is set in 15 acres (6ha) of spectacular gardens. Inside, the most notable features include the restored Rex Whistler Tent Room, the Moroccan Patio and the hexagonal library where the Treaty of Paris was signed after World War I. The Spencer Roberts mural room depicts over 300 animals and birds from South East Asia. Safari trailers journey through some of the animal paddocks during peak times; please telephone to check availability.
    Open all year, daily. Closed 25 Dec.

Set among Kentish orchards, this attractive downland village retains many half-timbered and brick houses and a fine row of cottages south of the churchyard.

Kent's county town, which stands in a countryside of orchards and hopfields on the River Medway, still has a real county town atmosphere, with the High Street leading up from the river, originally a wide market place, but later filled in to create parallel Bank Street. Both streets lead to the town centre with the town hall of 1763 and 1960s multi-storey blocks. Maidstone's oldest buildings are the 14th-century Archbishop's Palace, fronting the river, the great church of 1395 and the 15th-century Archbishop's stables.

LYMINGE
VILLAGE OFF A20, 4 MILES (6.5KM) N OF HYTHE

LYMPNE
VILLAGE ON B2067, 3 MILES (5KM) W OF HYTHE

Lympne Castle
TEL: 01303 267571

Port Lympne Wild Animal Park, Mansion & Garden
TEL: 01303 264647

LYNSTED
VILLAGE OFF A2, 3 MILES (5KM) SE OF SITTINGBOURNE

MAIDSTONE
TOWN OFF M20, 39 MILES (63KM) SE OF LONDON

Maidstone's position on the River Medway, historically an industrial highway, helped it to prosper. Fruit was sent to London; ragstone, Wealden iron, sand and timber were also transported. The Romans and Saxons were here; the Normans gave it its market in 1261; it developed a cloth-manufacturing industry, based on local flocks and fuller's earth, and was boosted by refugee Flemish weavers from the 1560s onwards. When the cloth industry died out, paper manufacture took over, and Maidstone remains an industrial centre.

The river is now a pleasure ground with boats and riverside walks. Maidstone hosts fairs including a carnival and river festival.

Leeds Castle

4 MILES (6.5KM), E AT JUNCTION 8 OF M20/A20

TEL: 01622 765400

Leeds Castle is not, as many would-be visitors might suppose, in the city of Leeds in West Yorkshire, but in the depths of the beautiful Kent countryside. It takes its name from its first owner, a man named Leed, or Ledian, who built himself a wooden castle in 857. Leed was the Chief Minister of the King of Kent, and in a time where a fall from grace or an attack by rival parties was a way of life, Leed was very wise in building a stronghold for his family on the two small islands in the lake formed by the River Len.

Leeds Castle, set in 500 acres (202ha) of landscaped parkland, has been beautifully restored

It is difficult to imagine what the original Leeds Castle must have looked like, especially when confronted by the grandeur of the building that stands on the two islands today. Edward I rebuilt the earlier Norman castle, providing it with a set of outer walls, a

barbican, and the curious 'gloriette', a D-shaped tower on the smaller of the two islands, which was altered extensively in the Tudor period. Much of Leeds Castle was restored and rebuilt in the 19th century, and many of the rooms are open to the public, all lavishly decorated, with superb collections of art and furniture.

Outside there are the Culpeper Flower Garden, the greenhouses, aviaries and vineyard, the 14th-century barbican and mill, the maze and grotto, and water and woodland gardens. Children especially love meeting the free-roaming waterfowl, which include peacocks as well as white and black swans.

The Fairfax Hall, a 17th-century tithe barn, is the venue for 'Kentish Evenings' each Saturday night (except during August) and is a fully licenced self-service restaurant during normal opening hours. The Terrace Room, with wonderful views of the castle and moat, operates a restaurant for visitors. There are also many special events throughout the year.

Open all year, daily.

Set in an Elizabethan manor house which has been much extended over the years, this museum houses a surprising and outstanding collection of fine and applied arts, including oil paintings and watercolours, furniture, Roman, Anglo-Saxon and medieval archeology, ceramics, costumes and a collection of Japanese art and artefacts. Natural history collections and displays relating to local industry are also featured, together with the Museum of the Queen's Own Royal West Kent Regiment. Apply for details of temporary exhibitions, workshops etc.

Open all year, daily. Closed 25–26 Dec.

Maidstone Museum & Art Gallery
Saint Faith's St (close to County Hall)
Tel: 01622 754497

This award-winning 40-acre (16-ha) open-air museum reflects changing times and lives in the 'Garden of England' over the last century. Here you will find the UK's last working oast house with a barn, granary, hoppers' huts, and waggon store house featuring fascinating exhibitions including the 'Darling Buds of May'. Other attractions include a livestock centre, craftsmen, hop, herb and kitchen gardens and orchards. Special events are held throughout the year.

Open Etr–Oct, daily.

Museum of Kent Life
Lock Ln, Sandling (from A229, follow signs for Aylesford)
Tel: 01622 763936

A wide array of horse-drawn carriages and vehicles is displayed in these late-medieval stables, which are interesting in themselves. The exhibits include state, official and private carriages, some of which are on loan from royal collections.

Open all year, daily. Closed 25–26 Dec.

Tyrwhitt Drake Museum of Carriages
The Archbishop's Stables, Mill St
Tel: 01622 754497

MARDEN

VILLAGE ON B2079, 7 MILES (11KM) S OF MAIDSTONE

The village, which lies among orchards and hopfields, has an attractive High Street of tile-hung and weatherboarded houses, and a medieval church (the belfry is topped with a pyramidal roof). The new village centre is by the station.

MARGATE

TOWN ON A28, 15 MILES (24KM) NE OF CANTERBURY

Margate, on the Isle of Thanet, is a popular and bustling seaside resort with 9 miles (14.5km) of sandy beach, safe swimming, arcades and funfairs, the Winter Gardens with a concert hall that seats 2,000, the Theatre Royal and the Tom Thumb Theatre with the world's smallest stage. The curious Grotto, chambers hollowed from the chalk and embedded with shells, possibly prehistoric, is beleived to be an 18th-century folly.

Margate was one of England's earliest coastal resorts, developed after 1753 when Benjamin Beale, a Margate Quaker, invented the bathing machine. The upper classes came to Margate to partake of the new and fashionable craze for sea bathing, making use of Beale's invention – a kind of waggon in which the bather was towed into the sea.

The first development, around Cecil Square (1769), was inland from the sea, behind the old fishing village, but soon London trippers were heading to Margate in their droves, first down the Thames and by sea and later by train, and building moved seawards as the 19th century progressed. Today the pier (1810), the parade and the little harbour separate the boisterous seaside sands and fun from the eastern cliffs and 19th-century terraces.

An engagingly dotty clock tower keeps a benevolent eye on Margate seafront

MATFIELD

VILLAGE ON B2160, 2 MILES (3KM) S OF PADDOCK WOOD

This attractive village has a lovely row of Georgian houses on the north side of the green, and a cricket pitch and duck pond.

Badsell Park Farm

CRITTENDEN RD (ON A228)
TEL: 01892 832223

A pleasant day in the country for all the family is offered at this attractive 180-acre (73-ha) fruit and arable farm. Children are able to handle young farm animals and domestic pets in the animal park and pet area. There are nature trails to follow in beautiful countryside, a butterfly house with live tropical species, a tropical ant house, picnic facilities and a play barn for toddlers and children up to eleven; outdoor play areas include Wendy houses, a fort, fire engine and tractor. An Information Room gives details of farming and wildlife, including live insect displays. Strawberries, apples and other fruit and vegetables can be picked in season. Special events are held during the year, telephone for details.

Open all year, daily.

Rising in the forest country of Sussex, near West Hoathly, the Medway flows into Kent past Tonbridge and Maidstone to its estuary at Rochester and on to Sheerness, where it joins the Thames estuary. Locks were built on the river as far upstream as Tonbridge. The Medway Court of Admiralty controls fishing in the lower reaches.

MEDWAY, RIVER
RIVER IN SE ENGLAND

This attractive village strung along a main road has its centre at Meopham Green, where the cricketing tradition goes back to the 18th century. The restored windmill of 1807 overlooks the green.

MEOPHAM
VILLAGE ON A227, 5 MILES (8KM) S OF GRAVESEND

There is modern and older housing in this village between the railway and the M20, where the church has a spectacular 15th-century west window.

MERSHAM
VILLAGE OFF A20, 3 MILES (5KM) SE OF ASHFORD

A grey little town on the highest point of the Isle of Sheppey, Minster looks out over the Thames and Medway estuaries. The double church consists of a nunnery church of 1130 and a later parish church.

MINSTER (MINSTER IN SHEPPEY)
TOWN ON B2008, 2 MILES (3KM) SE OF SHEERNESS

The village lies on the southern slopes of the Isle of Thanet overlooking Minster Marshes. It has a fine Norman church and a modern nunnery in the Norman buildings of the abbey grange.

MINSTER (MINSTER IN THANET)
VILLAGE OFF A253, 5 MILES (8KM) W OF RAMSGATE

One of the first nunneries in England was built on this site in the 7th century. The house was rebuilt in later centuries, but is still a religious community and is run by Benedictine nuns. The ruins of the old abbey and the cloisters are open to the public, and much of the Early English and Norman architecture can still be seen; there is one wing dating back to 1027.

Open all year, May–Sep daily; Oct–Apr mornings only.

Minster Abbey
TEL: 01843 821254

A little place in the rural Medway Valley, Nettlestead has a church (rebuilt in 1420) and a modern vineyard situated near the site of Roman vineyards.

NETTLESTEAD
VILLAGE ON B2015, 5 MILES (8KM) N OF PADDOCK WOOD

NEW ASH GREEN
VILLAGE OFF A227, 1 MILE (1.5KM) W OF MEOPHAM

This is a self-sufficient New Town begun in 1965, with a pedestrian shopping centre, school, playing fields and a church set among neighbourhoods of modern houses.

NEW ROMNEY
TOWN ON A259, 9 MILES (14KM) SW OF HYTHE

New Romney was the most important of the Cinque Ports until 1287, when a storm destroyed its harbour. Now the town is 1 mile (1.5km) from the sea, but Cinque Port documents are still kept in the guildhall. The grandeur of the big Norman church reflects the former greatness of the town in days when ships would anchor at the quay just below it. The High Street is pleasant, with many attractive Georgian houses. The local steam railway is built to one-third scale.

Romney, Hythe & Dymchurch Railway
TEL: 01797 362353 & 363256

Miniature railways have a fascination of their own, witnessed by the enduring popularity of the Romney, Hythe & Dymchurch Railway since it opened in 1927. Although the number of miniature railways has mushroomed since World War II, the concept of the Romney, Hythe & Dymchurch remains unique. The reason for this is largely due to its creator, Captain Jack Howey, who had the wealth to build a main line railway in miniature, with double track, substantial stations and powerful locomotives capable of a scale speed of 75mph (120kph).

A strong commercial case for such lavishness would be hard to make – no miniature railway of comparable length has been able to justify more than a single line, for example. But with the rental income from a good chunk of central Melbourne in Australia, Captain Howey did not have to worry about sceptical bank managers. To power his trains, Howey ordered nine steam locomotives, five based on the elegant Pacific design by Sir Nigel Gresley for the London & North Eastern Railway, two freight types for aggregate traffic that never materialised and a pair of Canadian-style Pacifics – Howey particularly enjoyed his railway holidays here.

The Duke of York, later King George VI, drove the first train into New Romney and the railway soon became well known as the World's Smallest Public Railway. It flourished during the 1930s and played its part in the defence of the Kent coast when an armoured train was built, sporting a couple of machine guns and an anti-tank rifle. Powered by a protected 4-8-2 *Samson*, it made regular forays from its dummy hill near Dymchurch.

Some economies were made on the railway as the popularity of holidays abroad eroded its traffic during the 1960s, but new management following Howey's death has helped to revive the railway's fortunes, and it remains one of the finest miniature railways in the world. Amongst many innovations is an observation car equipped with licensed bar.

Hythe is the largest resort on the line, with some fine Victorian hotels, and the terminal station still has the only original overall roof spanning its three platforms. It stands beside the Royal Military Canal, built to deter invasion by Napoleon. The station's size, coupled with the water tower, signal box, turntable and engine shed (now disused) help to create a main line atmosphere. The first section of the line is fringed by back gardens on one side and the remains of the canal on the other, before entering open country with wide views over the flat land of Romney Marsh. In the distance are the gently rising hills of Lympne. After many level crossings, open fields, a shallow cutting and a tunnel under a main road the train reaches the railway's headquarters at New Romney. The station has a popular model exhibition and impressive model railways. Although the station has a huge new roof spanning the running lines, elements of Howey's original station survive including the wooden clock tower. The final section of line traverses the broad expanse of shingle that surrounds the two nuclear power stations and two lighthouses at Dungeness. This area is a sanctuary for birds, moths, butterflies and rare plants.

Open daily Etr–Sep, also wknds Mar & Oct. For times apply to the Manager, R H & D R, New Romney, Kent.

In the sheds at New Romney station, the railway's headquarters

NEWCHURCH
VILLAGE OFF A259, 4 MILES
(6.5KM) N OF NEW ROMNEY

Newchurch is a Romney Marsh village with a wide scatter of isolated farms. The church has a spacious 15th-century tower and near by are deserted medieval villages.

NEWENDEN
VILLAGE ON A28, 5 MILES
(8KM) SW OF TENTERDEN

Situated on the River Rother, the boundary with Sussex, the village has an early 18th-century bridge and a church raised on a mound with a strange little tower and spire of 1859.

NEWNHAM
VILLAGE OFF A2, 5 MILES (8KM)
SW OF FAVERSHAM

The village consists of a long street of cottages amid orchards and parkland. Tudor Calico House recalls that Newnham was fomerly a centre of calico production.

NORE, THE
SANDBANK, OFF SHORE AT
SHEERNESS

This sandbank in the Thames estuary, 3 miles (5km) south-east of Sheerness, is marked by a Nore lightship. Traditionally, the name Nore refers to the western Thames estuary, a famous anchorage. Nore gave its name to the Nore Mutiny, a sailors' revolt of 1797.

NORTH FORELAND
HEADLAND OFF B2052, 1 MILE
(1.5KM) N OF BROADSTAIRS

These prominent white cliffs, the most easterly point in Kent and the south-western gate to the Thames estuary, have been crowned by a lighthouse since 1636.

NORTHBOURNE
VILLAGE OFF A256, 3 MILES
(5KM) W OF DEAL

This little country village lies on the chalk hills behind Deal. The church was built by monks of St Augustine's Abbey, Canterbury.

NORTHFLEET
TOWN ON A226, IMMEDIATELY
W OF GRAVESEND

This town on the Thames estuary was once famous for shipbuilding, and is where Portland cement was first developed. The Norman church contains a 14th-century oak screen, which is believed to be the oldest in Kent.

OARE
VILLAGE OFF A2, 1 MILE
(1.5KM) NW OF FAVERSHAM

Above Faversham Creek and the marshes that fringe the Swale, this is the site of a nature reserve occupying 170 acres (69ha) of open marsh, with rare plants and varied bird life.

OFFHAM
VILLAGE OFF A20, 2 MILES
(3KM) SW OF WEST MALLING

Offham is an attractive old village of local stone and timber cottages and 18th-century brick houses grouped around a green, on which stands a quintain, or tilting post.

OLD ROMNEY
VILLAGE ON A259, 2 MILES
(3KM) W OF NEW ROMNEY

This tiny Romney Marsh village, once an important port, now lies well inland as a result of many successful attempts to win land from the sea. It stands beside ancient Rhee Wall, an embankment and channel built by the Romans. St Clement's Church, which once overlooked the wharf, is remote from the village.

The village, which has many converted oast houses, lies among orchards above the River Stour on the North Downs Way.

OLD WIVES LEES
VILLAGE OFF A28, 5 MILES (8KM) W OF CANTERBURY

Ospringe is a street of attractive houses running along Roman Watling Street, with a church to the south-west. Maison Dieu (English Heritage), now housing a museum, was founded as a hospital in 1234.

OSPRINGE
HAMLET ON A2, IMMEDIATELY SW OF FAVERSHAM

An historic village in the Darent Gap, where the river finds its way through the North Downs, with a village pond and a 12th-century church by the wide green. The Castle of Otford, a ruinous tower and gatehouse of the Archbishop's Palace, was rebuilt splendidly in 1581. Becket's Well – said to have been created miraculously by the Archbishop – supplied water to the palace.

OTFORD
VILLAGE OFF A225, 3 MILES (5KM) N OF SEVENOAKS

The village pond at Otford

The village is virtually a Maidstone suburb, famous for its timber-framed houses, including Stoneacre (National Trust), a half-timbered 15th-century manor house with a cottage-style garden.

OTHAM
VILLAGE OFF A20, 3 MILES (5KM) SE OF MAIDSTONE

This low, hump-backed ridge, a former marshland island surrounded by watercourses, looks over the Rother Levels and Romney Marsh to the sea. Wittersham is its 'capital' (see page 90).

OXNEY, ISLE OF
DISTRICT IN THE ROTHER LEVELS, 5 MILES (8KM) N OF RYE

PAINTER'S FORSTAL
HAMLET OFF A251, 2 MILES (3KM) SW OF FAVERSHAM

The hamlet lies among the north Kent orchards. To the south is Belmont, an 18th-century mansion with a superb clock collection, mementoes of India, a walled garden, a pinetum and a folly.

PATRIXBOURNE
VILLAGE OFF A2, 3 MILES (5KM) SE OF CANTERBURY

The village is on Roman Watling Street in the valley of the intermittent Nailbourne stream, and is famous for its late Norman church among the trees in the village centre. Built in 1160, it has a porch with a finely carved doorway and tympanum, probably the work of Rochester Cathedral masons. Pretty Tudor-style houses, with overhanging gables and carved timbers, were built in the 1860s for tenants of Bilfrons, the demolished manor house.

PEGWELL BAY
BEACH OFF A256, SW OF RAMSGATE

This bay and beach at the southernmost point of the Isle of Thanet, has cliffs to the north and marsh to the south. It was the traditional landing place of Danes in AD 499 and St Augustine in AD 597.

PEMBURY
VILLAGE ON A21, 3 MILES (5KM) E OF TUNBRIDGE WELLS

Pembury is a busy sprawling residential place with a triangular green south of the village centre. Nearby Pembury Woods are excellent for walks.

PENSHURST PLACE
ON B2176, 4½ MILES (7KM) NW OF TUNBRIDGE WELLS
TEL: 01892 870307

The original part of Penshurst Place was built between 1340 and 1345 for Sir John de Pulteney, and although it was extended and modified by successive owners its magnificent baron's hall is superbly preserved. This was the heart of the medieval house, where the entire household lived beneath the wonderful chestnut-beamed roof; its central fireplace is still evident today. It is the oldest and the finest example of a medieval hall in the country.

Penshurst was closely connected with royalty, belonging at one time to Henry IV's third son, and later to Henry VIII. His son, Edward VI, gave the property to Sir William Sidney in 1552 and it is still the Sidney family home.

A great variety of architectural styles are incorporated in the building we see

today, although its battlemented exterior presents a unified face, and its series of interesting rooms provide a splendid backdrop for the superb furniture, crystal chandeliers, tapestries and works of art. There are family portraits everywhere, including one of that famous ancestor, Sir Philip Sidney, the great Elizabethan soldier, courtier and poet. A tremendous amount of restoration work has been carried out since World War II, when Penshurst was damaged by flying bombs, and it is as much a monument to the most recent generations of Sidneys as to its great figures of the past.

Open Etr–Oct daily.

(See also Cycle ride: Penshurst and Tudor Kent, page 62.)

Penshurst Place represents an intriguing blend of architectural styles

*T*he ride through this Tudor-influenced part of Kent is pleasant and historically interesting. Some short hills provide height for views over the surrounding countryside, and the suddenly encountered outcrops of rock seem out of place in this type of terrain. The route is on-road, with the option of a short bridleway run at the end for off-road cycling.

INFORMATION

Total Distance
16 miles (25.5km), with an optional 1½ miles (2.5km) off-road

Difficulty
Moderate

OS Maps
Landranger 1:50,000 sheet 188 (Maidstone & The Weald of Kent)

Tourist Information
Tonbridge, tel: 01732 770929

Cycle Hire
The Secret Garden Bike Hire Co, 113 Barden Road, Tonbridge, tel: 01732 367233

Nearest Railway Station
Penshurst (2 miles/3km)

Refreshments
There are plenty of facilities in Penshurst, including the Fir Tree House Tea Rooms, Quaintways, The Leicester Arms pub, and the Spotted Dog. Pubs on the route

include The Fountain at Cowden (no facilities for children), The Kentish Horse at Markbeech, The Henry VIII at Hever, The Wheatsheaf at Bough Beech, and the attractive Castle Inn at Chiddingstone. There is a restaurant and café at Hever Castle, and the Village Tea Rooms at Chiddingstone.

START

Penshurst village lies between Sevenoaks and Tunbridge Wells,

Chiddingstone village

west of Tonbridge on the B2176. Park with care in the layby on the B2176 opposite Penshurst Place.

DIRECTIONS

1. From the parking place, go to the centre of Penshurst and turn right along the B2188, signposted 'Tunbridge Wells'. In ½ mile (1km) turn right, signposted to Chiddingstone Hoath, and continue for ¼ mile (0.5km) to

Cycle ride

reach a T-junction. Turn right, towards Chiddingstone Hoath, and in ½ mile (1km) bear left, signposted 'Markbeech/ Cowden'.

2. Continue, and in 1 mile (1.5km) bear left again towards Cowden. Pass through Horseshoe Green and go under the railway bridge. Cross the B2026 and enter the village of Cowden. Pass the church and take the first

turning right. Follow the road away from the village, and pass Waystrode Manor. Continue for 1 mile (1.5km) and bear right to meet the B2026 again at the Queen's Arms pub.

3. Continue straight ahead, signposted to Markbeech and Hever Castle. After 1 mile (1.5km), in Markbeech turn left into Uckfield Lane, by The Kentish Horse pub. Go down the hill, and

The village of Chiddingstone is a favourite period setting for films

after 1½ miles (2.5km) turn right opposite a bus shelter, signposted to Hever Castle and Penshurst, and continue into Hever village. Follow the road left, to pass Hever Castle on the right.

4. Continue on this road, signposted 'Bough Beech', for 1½ miles (2.5km), meeting the

63

railway line, and bear right to join the B2027 at The Wheatsheaf pub. Go straight on, and immediately after Chequers Garage, turn right. After 1 mile (1.5km) turn left at the crossroads into Chiddingstone village.

5. Proceed through the village and in ½ mile (1km) take the right fork to pass through Weller's Town. After a further ½ mile (1km) look out for a bridleway on the left by Lew Cross Farm.
Turn left here and bear left again at Wat Stock, following the Eden Valley Walk back to the car park at Penshurst.

(*Alternatively*, go straight on at Lew Cross Farm to Hoath Corner. Turn left at The Rock pub and continue, to meet the outward route at Chiddingstone Hoath. Turn left and left again following the signs to retrace the route to Penshurst.)

PLACES OF INTEREST

Penshurst
The village lies between two rivers, Medway and Eden, and has retained its character although overshadowed by the grandeur of Penshurst Place. Penshurst Place, home of the

A view of rolling countryside from the tower of Penshurst church

Sidney family since 1552, fell into ruin and was restored by later generations of the family during the 19th century. The gardens date from the 14th century and the house can be visited. The church enclosed within the grounds is also of interest particularly for its entrance between some cottages.

(See also page 60.)

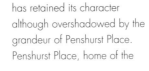

WHAT TO LOOK OUT FOR

The well-kept timber-framed and tile-hung houses give an air of prosperity to this part of Kent. Azaleas and rhododendrons provide the colour in early summer and the many trees attract an abundance of woodland birds, including woodpeckers. The route passes some unusual rock formations including the famous Chiding Stone in Chiddingstone.

Cycle ride

Hever Castle

This moated 13th-century castle is renowned for its connection with Anne Boleyn. In 1903 it was restored and beautifully furnished by the Astors, and is now a major tourist attraction and a conference centre. The adjoining Tudor 'village' is used as guest suites for conference delegates. The grounds have a 35-acre (14ha) lake, 30 acres (12ha) of gardens, including the unique Italian garden with a collection of Roman statues, and a maze.

(See also page 44.)

Chiddingstone

Chiddingstone has retained its historic charm and has been used as a location for film settings. There are many examples of 16th- and 17th-century architecture with half-timbered and tile-hung frontages to the houses. The most interesting of these is The Castle Inn, which dates from the 15th century or earlier. The village was acquired by the National Trust in 1939 except for the fine Church of St Mary's. The Georgian Chiddingstone Castle is a remodelled 17th-century ironmaster's house.

(See also page 24.)

A colourful corner of the gardens at Hever Castle

PLAXTOL
VILLAGE OFF A227, 5 MILES (8KM) N OF TONBRIDGE

This is a large hilltop village with a long village street, a lovely group of cottages around the church, and a working forge making gates and weathervanes.

Old Soar Manor
TEL: 01892 890651

Built by the famous Kentish family, the Culpepers, in 1290, and amazingly intact, the solar, chapel, lavatorium and barrel-vaulted undercroft of Old Soar (English Heritage and National Trust) is joined to a lovely Georgian red-brick farmhouse. An ancient oak door displays 'graffiti' through the ages.
   Open Apr–Sep, daily.

PLUCKLEY
VILLAGE OFF A20, 3 MILES (5KM) SW OF CHARING

The village is situated on the serene slopes of greensand hills overlooking the Weald, the old centre is around the church and there are modern houses beyond. Pluckley is famed for its many ghosts; about a dozen are said to haunt the area.

RAMSGATE
TOWN ON A253, 15 MILES (24KM) NE OF CANTERBURY

Fishing boats and pleasure craft in Ramsgate harbour

A seaside resort, fishing village and cross-Channel terminal, Ramsgate has been a harbour with an eye on the Continent since Roman times. The little circular harbour, built out of the cliffed eastern coast of Thanet, is surrounded by pleasant Georgian terraces, with Victorian development along the front and the Royal Esplanade with its amusement parks and pavilion. Today commercial vessels, the fishing

fleet and pleasure craft patronise the harbour near the large marina. The cross-Channel ferry terminal (1981) is to the south. Every August Ramsgate holds a harbour Heritage Festival.

Most of Ramsgate's worthwhile architecture went up between 1810 and 1850: crescents, terraces and one or two squares, all in softly coloured brick with plenty of cast-iron balconies – a Ramsgate speciality. The harbour became 'royal' in 1827 when George IV stayed there, the same year St George's, the parish church, was built with its 137-ft (52-m) high tower. Ramsgate is dominated by St Augustine's Church and Abbey (Roman Catholic): Pugin's masterpiece of 1850, externally bleak, internally magnificent. On the hilltop near by is a model village in Tudor style – a 1953 dream of idyllic England.

The Ramsgate Maritime Museum is housed in the early 19th-century Clock House, a Grade II Listed building, and contains four galleries depicting various aspects of the maritime heritage of the east Kent area. The adjacent restored dry dock and floating exhibits from the museum's historic ship collection include the steam tug *Cervia* and the Dunkirk 'little ship' motor yacht *Sundowner*.

Open Apr–Sep, daily; Oct–Mar, certain days.

Maritime Museum
Clock House, Pier Yard,
Royal Harbour
Tel: 01843 587765

The museum tells the story of Ramsgate in days gone by with paintings and photographs of Royal Harbour, churches, breweries, pubs, shops, Ramsgate personalities and holiday souvenirs.

Open all year, daily. Closed Xmas & BHs.

Ramsgate Museum
Ramsgate Library, Guildford
Lawn
Tel: 01843 593532

The villagers, and the village, moved inland in the 17th century as a result of the encroching sea. The twin 12th-century towers ('The Sisters') of the church they left behind now dominate the headland in Reculver Country Park, 91 acres (37ha) of grassy hilltop, seashore and woodland, renowned for bird-watching.

(See also Walk: Reculver's Sea Bed Paths, page 68.)

RECULVER
Village off A299, 3 miles
(5km) E of Herne Bay

The Roman *Regulbium* was one of the forts built during the 3rd century to defend the Saxon shore. The fort (English Heritage) was in good condition until the 18th century, when erosion of the cliffs on which it stands caused part of the walls to collapse into the sea below.

During the 7th century an Anglo-Saxon church was built on the site, and its floor plan can be traced. The church was extended and, during the 12th century, the Normans built on a west front and two huge towers. These are still almost intact, providing a mariners' landmark.

Open all year, daily.

Reculver Towers & Roman
Fort
3 miles (5km) E of Herne Bay
Tel: 01227 366444

*T*his is an unusual walk around part of the old sea bed which separated Kent from the Isle of Thanet. The paths, built high above the silted channel, offer easy walking and afford fine views in all directions – perfect for bird-watching.

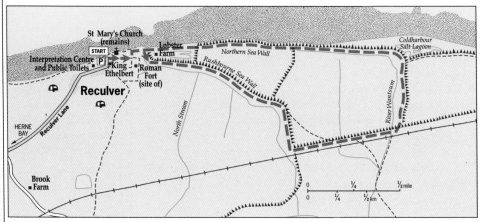

Grid ref: TQ697224
INFORMATION

The walk is 3½ (5.5km) miles long.
Level, easy ground.
No road walking.
No stiles.
Pub at Reculver serves bar meals; children are welcome.
Grassy area within ruins and by paths suitable for picnics.
One café.
Interpretation Centre for information.

START

Reculver is 1 mile (1.5km) east of Herne Bay, just off the A299 Thanet Way. Start the walk from the King Ethelbert pub. There is parking near the end of the road, opposite the pub.

DIRECTIONS

Turn towards the sea and walk up the path leading to the ruins of Reculver's church. The path runs between the south side of the church and the grassed site of a Roman fort. Where the path runs down into the old shoreline go left towards the present seashore. Follow the sea wall and between crossing a stream and reaching a gate turn right to walk on to a high bank. The bank, known as the Rushborne Sea Wall, turns left around the back of Lobster Farm and runs in a south-easterly direction deep into the old channel. Continue, ignoring any turnings back to the sea. Look out for occasional waymark posts, and later follow the bank as it turns sharply south to reach the railway. Do not cross the tracks, but turn left along the high path running parallel to the line. Stay by the railway until crossing the River Wantsum then immediately turn left down the slope to follow a sea-level track alongside water flowing towards the sea. The path rises to meet the sea wall at Coldharbour Salt Lagoon. Turn left and follow the wide path back to the ruins of St Mary's Church which can be seen 1½ miles (2.5km) away.

Walk

Reculver

Once this was Kent's most north-easterly point – when the Romans built a fort here in AD 43 the sea was nearly a mile (1.5km) away; by 1809 the cliff was so close that the villagers panicked and moved over a mile (1.5km) inland, building a new church there. The two 12th-century towers at Reculver are the remains of the original church. When the villagers too were forced to leave by the encroaching sea, they left the two towers as landmarks for shipping.

(See also page 67.)

Wantsum Channel

The Isle of Thanet was once separated from Reculver on the mainland by a tidal channel a third of a mile wide. For centuries most crossings were made to the south where the Roman road ran to the sea opposite Sarre. By 1500 a programme of drainage, together with natural silting, had prevented shipping from using the channel, which has now shrunk to a drainage dyke.

WHAT TO LOOK OUT FOR

The marsh is a resting place for hundreds of migratory birds. Kestrels may be seen, and there are reed and sedge warblers in the reed-beds in summer. Along the shore, terns fish in summer and Brent geese arrive from Siberia in autumn. The grazing marshes and fields inland are renowned for sightings of birds of prey in winter, including hen harrier, merlin and rough-legged buzzard. Along the sea wall clovers and other wild flowers attract butterflies, and common lizards bask in the sun.

The twin towers of Reculver's ruined church

Goat's-beard

RICHBOROUGH CASTLE
2 MILES (3KM) N OF
SANDWICH OFF A256
TEL: 01304 612013

Now landlocked in the Kent countryside, Richborough Castle (English Heritage) once stood on the coast, the bridgehead from which the Romans launched their invasion in AD 43. The foundations of the great monumental archway, built to mark the conquest of Britain, can still be seen today. The remains of Richborough's massive fortified wall and defensive ditches convey a vivid impression of the power of the Roman empire, and the museum contains finds from the site.

Open Apr–Nov, daily.

RINGWOULD
VILLAGE ON A258, 3 MILES
(5KM) S OF DEAL

Ringwould is a pleasant old place with pretty cottages above the Deal and Dover road. The church, perched high up looking out to sea, has a west tower topped with a jaunty cupola.

ROCHESTER
CITY OFF M2, 28 MILES
(45KM) E OF LONDON

The Romans founded Rochester where Watling Street, their great road from the Channel ports to London, bridged the tidal River Medway. Historically the road has brought travellers to the city, including medieval Canterbury pilgrims and stagecoach passengers.

The Saxons founded the cathedral, consecrated in AD 604, the second oldest in England. The Normans rebuilt it from 1077, including the spectacular west doorway. Additions were made in the 12th and 14th centuries, with rebuilding after Civil War damage. The magnificent nave has a superb oak roof supported by carved angels. The close is informal and intimate, and the nearby monastic ruins are set in gardens. The park, The Vines, was probably the monastic vineyard.

The Normans saw the city's strategic value and built a castle. The present castle (English Heritage), which dominates the hill behind the cathedral, dates from 1130. Within the walls are gardens and the massive 120-ft (36-m) high keep with walls 12ft (4m) thick.

Rochester's partly pedestrianised High Street has changed little in the last century; the buildings are mostly Georgian, or have Georgian façades. The shops are small, and the scale is human. The former Corn Exchange, 1705, bears a great clock on an ornamental bracket protruding from its façade, while the old Guildhall, now a museum, is a splendid building of 1687 crowned by a copper weathervane of 1780 in the shape of a full-rigged ship.

Charles Dickens knew Rochester well, and it appears in many of his books, notably *Great Expectations*. There is a Charles Dickens Centre and a Dickens' Festival in May/June. Other festivals include the Chimney Sweeps

Picturesque Dickens' chalet, Rochester

(May) and the Carnival and Regatta (July). Rochester has craft and antiques shops, sports and leisure facilities and riverside gardens.

Eastgate House is a fine late Tudor building which contains an audio-visual presentation of Charles Dickens' life and works. There are two new features – a dramatic tableau with state-of-the-art special effects based upon a famous painting *Dickens' Dream,* in which many of the great author's most famous characters appear to him whilst he sleeps in his study; and an audio-visual theatre showing presentations of Dickens, his life and works and his connections with the Medway Towns (available for groups booked in advance only). Eastgate House appeared as Westgate House in *Pickwick Papers* and The Nun's House in *Edwin Drood.* The garden houses Dickens' chalet from Gad's Hill Place, Higham, which he used as a study in fine weather.
    Open all year, daily. Closed Xmas.

Charles Dickens Centre
EASTGATE HOUSE, HIGH ST
TEL: 01634 844176

Built in 1687, the Guildhall has magnificent decorated plaster ceilings. Recent refurbishment of the adjoining later wing has resulted in new displays of local history from prehistoric times to the beginning of the 19th century. There is a feature gallery on the subject of the Medway Prison Hulks. The fine adjacent building, constructed in 1909 as offices for the Conservators of the River Medway, houses the museum's 19th-century collections.
    Open all year, daily. Closed Xmas.

Guildhall Museum
HIGH ST
TEL: 01634 848717

The magnificent Norman keep at Rochester has seen more than its share of battles and sieges, but perhaps the most famous one was in 1215. Shortly after the barons forced King John to sign the Magna Carta, he turned against them in a bitter war. Rochester Castle (English Heritage) was held for the barons, and John laid siege to it with incredible ferocity. The siege lasted for about seven weeks, during which time those in the castle were reduced to a diet of horsemeat and water. Meanwhile, John kept a constant barrage of missiles from crossbows and ballistas (stone-throwing machines), and began to dig a tunnel under the keep itself. Part of the keep collapsed, but the defenders bravely fought on. Those men who could no longer fight were sent out, where it is said John had their hands and feet cut off. But Rochester finally fell, and the defenders were imprisoned.
    Building on the keep started in about 1127, and it is one of the largest in England. Its walls soar to 113ft (34m) and are up to 12ft (3.5m) thick. Although this was first and foremost a defensive building, there are some beautifully carved archways and windows.
    Open all year, daily. Closed Xmas.

Rochester Castle
ROCHESTER, 10 MILES (16KM) N OF MAIDSTONE (BY ROCHESTER BRIDGE (A2), JUNC 1 M2, JUNC 2 M25)
TEL: 01634 402276

From one of the Weald's prettiest villages, this walk goes through the churchyard to a wood where there is a glimpse of the original walled garden which featured in Frances Hodgson Burnett's The Secret Garden.

Grid ref: TQ316843

INFORMATION

The walk is just under 2 miles (3km) long.

Several high stiles, and the path may be muddy in places.

Dogs will need to be kept on lead in the fields.

Pub (The Bull Inn) in Rolvenden for bar meals has a small garden; children welcome.

Layne's Green suitable for picnics.

START

Rolvenden is 2 miles (3km) south-west of Tenterden on the A28. Start the walk from Rolvenden church at the south end of the main street. There is some parking by the lych-gate. Avoid the narrow lane by the war memorial.

DIRECTIONS

At the main church door go right along the grass path at the side of the tower and, keeping to the right-hand side of the churchyard, follow a track to a kissing-gate (leave on the latch or sheep may get through). Bear half-left down the line of oaks and climb up to a redundant stile. Keep ahead past three sycamore trees and head

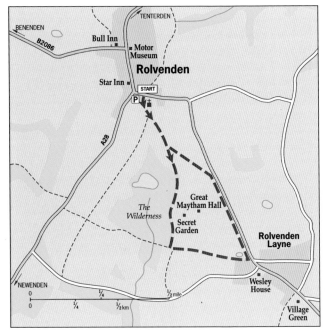

towards the stile on the edge of the wood, known as The Wilderness, following a path through the trees. On crossing the old Great Maytham driveway (gate on the left) there is the first glimpse of the walled 'secret garden' on the left. After another view the path runs gently downhill to a stile. Turn sharp left to cross another stile and proceed along the side of a field. At the far end go over a stile (which has a dog

gate) and follow an enclosed path. Beyond another stile, by a pond, continue in the same direction and go through two farm gates to the road at Rolvenden Layne.

Turn left, taking the pavement on the far side, to reach Great Maytham's main entrance. Continue on the road for a few yards to find a stile (with a dog flap) set back in the trees on the left. Once in the field, pass two

ROLVENDEN'S SECRET GARDEN

holly bushes and touch the field corner on the left. Keep ahead to pass between two tree clumps and join the outward path back to Rolvenden church.

Rolvenden

Rolvenden has a wide main street lined with weather-boarded cottages. Its church was built by monks from Canterbury in around 1220 and has remained largely unchanged since 1480. The village, which has more than once been declared 'the best kept' in Kent, is known for its locally produced Korker sausages, invented in the

The church at Rolvenden

WHAT TO LOOK OUT FOR

Rabbits abound in the field by the wood. In the churchyard, which is left partly wild, and on the woodland path there are summer wayside plants including common knapweed, spear thistle, creeping thistle, oxeye daisy and yarrow.

butcher's shop opposite The Bull. Rolvenden has a small motor museum.

(See also page 74.)

Rolvenden Layne

When fire swept through Rolvenden in 1665 the population moved here to start a second village. Already here was the Tudor house where John

Wesley preached in the late 18th century.

Great Maytham

Frances Hodgson Burnett rented this house in 1898 and a blocked-up door in the old walled garden inspired her to write *The Secret Garden*. After her departure in 1907 the mansion was rebuilt by Edwin Lutyens.

ROLVENDEN

*VILLAGE ON A28, 3 MILES
(5KM) SW OF TENTERDEN*

This is a large, prosperous village in orchard and hop country with a pleasant street of white weatherboarded and tile-hung houses.

(See also Walk: Rolvenden's Secret Garden, page 72.)

CM Booth Collection of Historic Vehicles

*FALSTAFF ANTIQUES,
63 HIGH ST (ON A28)
TEL: 01580 241234*

The collection is made up of historic vehicles and other items of interest connected with transport. The main feature is the unique collection of three-wheel Morgan cars, dating from 1913. Also here is the only known Humber tri-car of 1904; and items include a 1929 Morris van, a 1936 Bampton caravan, motorcycles and bicycles. There is also a toy and model car display.

Open all year most days. Closed 25 Dec.

ROMNEY MARSH

*SCENIC AND HISTORIC REGION,
W OF DYMCHURCH*

This large tract of rich pastureland was a bay of the sea even in historical times. It was protected from the sea by a huge earth embankment, Dymchurch Wall, between Hythe and New Romney, and backed by the old cliff-line and the Royal Military Canal, which

*The Pines garden at
St Margaret's at Cliffe is a
haven of rural calm*

was constructed in 1807. Reclamation was begun by the Romans, and continued until the 19th century. Romney Marsh was also the name given to a breed of sheep noted for its hardy qualities. The area was associated with 'owlers' — wool smugglers — in the 18th century.

This little town with weatherboarded houses is perched above St Margaret's Bay, a secluded resort and beach on the Channel shore approached down a steep cliff road near South Foreland. The Pines gardens take advantage of the warm micro-climate at the cliff foot with specimen trees, shrubs and lakes. This is the traditional starting point for cross-Channel swimmers, as it is the nearest point to France.

Cottages huddle together in this small place, remote and lonely on the flats of Romney Marsh. The unrestored 13th-century church stands by a bridge over a drainage channel.

Situated away from main roads, this is a delightful Thanet village with many brick cottages and houses in its centre.

Sandhurst is a village of weatherboarded houses straggling along a main road, with a delightful secluded green tucked away from the bustle, and a church away from the village on a hilltop to the south.

Sandwich was founded by the Saxons on the coast at the mouth of the River Stour. Since then the river has silted up and Sandwich is 2 miles (3km) inland, with fields and golf courses juxtaposed between it and the sea. An original Cinque Port, Sandwich was one of England's most important naval bases, yet by the 15th century it was no longer even a harbour, but a cloth-manufacturing town, its continued prosperity coming from refugee Flemish weavers who settled there. When the cloth industry declined Sandwich became an exclusive golfing resort, with the Royal St George's Golf Club between the town and Sandwich Bay, where there is a nature reserve.

Today it is a quiet little market town with narrow streets and alleys radiating from Cattle Market, the central square with its Elizabethan town hall housing the museum. Strand Street, which runs along the former seafront, now riverside, is full of timber-framed buildings including the magnificent Weaver's Hall and the King's Arms. Two of the town gates survive: massive Barbican Gate to the north, leading to the swing bridge over the river, and Fisher Gate (1384) overlooking the quay.

(See also: A Picnic at Sandwich Quay, page 76.)

ST MARGARET'S AT CLIFFE
SMALL TOWN OFF A258, 4 MILES (6.5KM) NE OF DOVER

ST MARY IN THE MARSH
VILLAGE OFF A259, 2 MILES (3KM) N OF NEW ROMNEY

ST NICHOLAS AT WADE
VILLAGE OFF A28, 6 MILES (9.5KM) SW OF MARGATE

SANDHURST
VILLAGE ON A268, 5 MILES (8KM) SW OF CRANBROOK

SANDWICH
TOWN ON A257, 11 MILES (17.5KM) E OF CANTERBURY

*W*ithin easy strolling distance of the centre of Sandwich, the oldest of the Cinque Ports, the quay and its adjacent grassy area alongside the River Stour form the perfect place to relax with a picnic, prior to exploring the narrow streets lined with attractive period buildings, browsing the specialist shops, or visiting the town's museums.

HOW TO GET THERE

From Canterbury (A257), or Dover and Deal (A258), follow the one-way system through the town centre to the bridge over the River Stour. Turn right beside the Bell Hotel for the free car park on the quay.

From Ramsgate, cross the Stour and turn immediately left to the car park. The picnic site is situated on the far side of the parking area.

FACILITIES

Riverside meadow beyond the car park has an adjacent, fenced children's playground, located away from the river across a traffic-free access road.
Tennis courts, riverside walk along the well-maintained path Stour Valley Walk to Sandwich Bay (2 miles/3km long).
Toilets, and nearby tearooms, pubs and restaurants.

THE SITE

The quay offers a convenient parking area and peaceful picnic place, with wooden benches and plenty of grass for laying out rugs along the willow-fringed riverbank. Active youngsters will enjoy the excellent safe playground. The information board notes that Sandwich was one of the best medieval trading ports in the country, with large ships tying up at the quay before the wide estuary began silting up in the 16th century.

RIVERSIDE ATTRACTIONS

Visitors can stroll along the

Sandwich quay

quayside where a range of old boats, including Thames-style barges and houseboats, float quietly up and down with the tide, or take a river-bus trip on the Stour to the small nature reserve of Gazen Salts, and beyond to the Roman ruins of Richborough Castle (English Heritage) and the museum which displays finds from the site.

Further along the Stour Valley Walk, a level path that tracks the silted-up river, you can see a variety of bird life, including herons and migrant warblers, while the town wall path leads on to The Bulwarks, which were part of the original walled defences.

HISTORIC BUILDINGS

Sandwich is a town perfect to walk in, whether on the ramparts or through the narrow, twisting streets, with their overhanging timber-framed buildings. A short walk through Fisher Gate (1385), the only remaining medieval town gate, and along Quay Lane into Fisher Street brings you to the heart of the town, where many period buildings survive.

Outstanding among these are the 16th-century Guildhall, with its museum and carved, panelled courtroom, the 12th-century parish church with its fine Norman arcaded tower, and the Barbican, a splendid gatehouse overlooking

Tubs of colourful petunias adorn the spacious town square at Sandwich

the bridge, built by Henry VIII in 1539 as part of his coastal defence system. Strand Street reputedly contains more half-timbered houses than any other street in England.

(See also page 75.)

CLOSE BY

Pegwell Bay and Sandwich Bay are good for wildlife enthusiasts. White Mill, a smock-mill built in 1760 on the edge of Sandwich, contains original machinery and houses a folk museum.

SARRE
VILLAGE ON A28, 4 MILES
(6.5KM) SW OF BIRCHINGTON

Sarre is a small place with a large windmill on the edge of marshes, between the mainland and the Isle of Thanet. It was the site of an important harbour and ferry when the marshes were an arm of the sea.

SEVENOAKS
TOWN OFF A21, 6 MILES
(10KM) N OF TONBRIDGE

A pleasant country town 500ft (152m) up, overlooking the Weald, Sevenoaks stands at the gates of its great house, Knole (National Trust), set in a superb deer park. The High Street is very attractive with many 17th- to 19th-century houses. There is a museum, theatre, a famous school and a wildfowl reserve. Sevenoaks hosts a summer festival.

Knole
S END OF SEVENOAKS,
E OF A225
TEL: 01732 450608

Thomas Bourchier, Archbishop of Canterbury, bought Knole in 1456 and set about transforming it from a simple medieval manor house into his palace; a century later the house was given to Henry VIII who extended it to even grander proportions. In the middle of the 16th century Knole was given to Thomas Sackville by Queen Elizabeth I; the Sackvilles kept the house for ten generations. Thomas lavished a fortune on the refurbishment and decoration of the house. Today, thanks to him, it is the largest house in England. He employed an army of builders, plasterers, upholsterers and glaziers including 300 specially imported Italians; where most Elizabethan houses had one Long Gallery, Knole has three. The 13 state rooms open to the public are rich in architectural detail from the 17th and 18th centuries. They house a collection of historical portraits, including works by Gainsborough and Van Dyck, and an outstanding collection of 17th-century English furniture which adds to their beauty. Outside, 26 acres (10.5ha) of gardens contain formal walks among the flower beds and fruit trees while beyond the encircling walls are further acres of undulating pasture and parkland open by courtesy of Lord Sackville. Knole is in the care of the National Trust.

Open Etr–Oct certain days. Garden open first Wed in month, May–Sep.

SEVENOAKS WEALD
VILLAGE OFF A21, 3 MILES
(5KM) SW OF SEVENOAKS

This is a pretty village with a little green in wooded countryside, with a church of 1820 and Else's Farm, where poet Edward Thomas lived in the early 20th century.

SHEERNESS
TOWN ON A249, 10 MILES
(16KM) N OF SITTINGBOURNE

Sheerness, a dockyard town, deep-water port and seaside resort lies on the extreme north-west tip of the Isle of Sheppey at the confluence of the rivers Thames and Medway. The Promenade, resplendent with gardens and amusements, overlooks the busy Thames estuary and beach. The deep-water container port near the site of naval dockyards (1665-1961) is now a trading estate.

An island off the north Kent coast, 9 miles (14.5km) long, 5 miles (8km) broad, Sheerness is separated from the mainland by the Swale and Medway estuary. The main towns are Sheerness and Queenborough, with access by Kingsferry Bridge over the Swale. A ridge runs east-west along the island, dropping north to the Thames estuary as cliffs. To the south are reclaimed marshes broken by creeks, and the important nature reserve of the Swale, which is rich in birdlife.

The village has a pleasant main street of delightful Kentish houses of many eras. Tudor Sissinghurst Castle, with its gardens created by Vita Sackville-West, is 1 mile (1.5km) north-east of the village.
(See also Walk: From Cranbrook to Sissinghurst, page 26.)

Deer graze in the grounds of Knole, England's largest house

SHEPPEY, ISLE OF
Island on A249, off N coast of Kent

SISSINGHURST
Village on A229, 1 mile (1.5km) NE of Cranbrook

SITTINGBOURNE
*TOWN ON A2, 8 MILES
(13KM) E OF GILLINGHAM*

Sittingbourne is an industrial town with a long history as a market town and staging post. It lies near Roman Watling Street on a creek off the Swale in the heart of Kentish cherry orchards. In the Middle Ages this was a stopping place for pilgrims to Canterbury and had a thriving market. Today, paper-manufacture and fruit-preserving and packing are the main industries.

Dolphin Sailing Barge Museum
*CROWN QUAY LN
(N ON A2)
TEL: 01795 423215*

The museum is dedicated to presenting the history of the Thames spritsail sailing barge, many of which were built along the banks of Milton Creek. Tools of the trade, photographs of many barges and associated artefacts can be seen at the barge yard along with the sailing barge *Cumbria*. Privately owned barges are repaired – there is a forge, shipwright's shop and sail loft.

Open Etr–Oct, Sun & BHs.

SMALL HYTHE
*HAMLET ON B2082, 2 MILES
(3KM) S OF TENTERDEN*

A charming roadside hamlet to the north of the Isle of Oxney, Small Hythe was originally a port for Tenterden. Excellent buildings include Smallhythe Place, once the home of actress Ellen Terry.

Smallhythe Place
*3 MILES (5KM) S OF TENTERDEN
ON B2082
TEL: 01580 762334*

Once a Tudor harbour master's house, this half-timbered, 16th-century building became Dame Ellen Terry's last home. It is now a museum of Ellen Terry memorabilia and is in the care of the National Trust. The barn has been made into a theatre and is open most days courtesy of the Barn Theatre Company. There is a charming cottage garden, including Ellen Terry's rose garden.

Open Apr–Oct, certain afternoons.

SMARDEN
*VILLAGE OFF A262, 7 MILES
(11KM) N OF TENTERDEN*

An old Wealden wool village, Smarden has a particularly attractive high street, with white weatherboarded and half-timbered houses on either side. The Dragon House, next to the village pump, was built in 1331 for a family of Dutch weavers brought over by Edward III to weave broadcloth. Chessenden is a good Wealden hall house, built in 1462. Further evidence of the village's prosperity as a cloth town is to be found near the church in the two big half-timbered houses built by wealthy clothiers. The excellent cloth hall is dated to about 1420; the hoist that was used for lifting bales of cloth into the loft still hangs from the gable at the west end.

Next door, Matthew Hartnup's house has his name carved on it; it is probably older than the 1671 date shown. The church dates from the 14th century, it has a 15th-century tower and is built of local Bethersden marble. It is called the 'Barn of Kent' because of its surprising width and absence of aisles to support the 36-ft (11-m) span of its wooden roof, a rare occurrence in medieval churches. Another

ɡazetteer

Smarden's church overlooks the white weatherboarded buildings in the high street

rarity is the oven for baking communion wafers, near the high altar. Smarden continued to thrive as a weaving town, with a weekly market, until the 19th century when hops were introduced to the area. Oast houses in the village date from this time.

An industrial place on the west bank of the River Medway, Snodland is dominated by cement works and papermills. Steep wooded hills climb up behind the village.

This chalk headland, the eastern extremity of the White Cliffs of Dover, guards the strait. There are two lighthouses; the older (1843) is now owned by the National Trust, and was used in 1898 for the first radio navigation aid.

Speldhurst is an attractive residential village situated in the wooded hills, with an old pub, and a notable Victorian church containing ten splendid colourful stained-glass windows which were designed by Burne-Jones.

SNODLAND
VILLAGE ON A228, 5 MILES (8KM) NW OF MAIDSTONE

SOUTH FORELAND
HEADLAND OFF A258, 3 MILES (5KM) NE OF DOVER

SPELDHURST
VILLAGE OFF A264, 2 MILES (3KM) NW OF TUNBRIDGE WELLS

A row of particularly fine Tudor houses in Staplehurst

STAPLEHURST
VILLAGE ON A229, 6 MILES (10KM) N OF CRANBROOK

This is a pleasant old village with a particularly fine main street with raised pavements and lovely Kentish houses, including an 18th-century post office and half-timbered Fuller House.

STONE (STONE-CUM-EBONY)
VILLAGE OFF B2080, 2 MILES (3KM) SW OF APPLEDORE

Perched on the former seacliff of the Isle of Oxney, this little village has a Roman altar preserved in its church.

STONE STREET
ROMAN ROAD

This Roman road is one of several radiating from the major route centre, Canterbury, heading south to Lympne, an important Roman port. It is largely followed by the B2068.

STOUR, RIVER
RIVER, COMBINING GREAT STOUR AND LITTLE STOUR

Rising near Hythe, the River Stour flows 40 miles (64.5km) across Kent past Canterbury to Stourmouth; it then continues across marshlands past Sandwich to Pegwell Bay and the sea.

STROOD
TOWN ON A2, ACROSS RIVER MEDWAY FROM ROCHESTER

Overlooking the River Medway, this big old town is joined to Rochester by a bridge which carries Roman Watling Street. The town was frequented by Canterbury pilgrims in the Middle Ages; several hospitals were built for them. High Street is narrow and winding and the town is hemmed in by industry. The 14th-century church (founded pre-1193) was rebuilt in 1812 by Sir Robert Smirke, his first work.

The village, which lies on the River Stour, was largely rebuilt after bomb damage in World War II. It retains a Norman church tower and huge old weatherboarded and brick barn.

This is a characterful village with a square and several delightful houses strung out along the road between Sevenoaks and Westerham.

This busy industrial village, by the River Darant, is on an ancient site with St John's Jerusalem Garden (National Trust) beside a moated house, originally a commandery of the Knights Hospitallers.

Set among orchards on the steep south-facing Quarry Hills, this charming village enjoys superb views over the Weald from the attractive High Street.

Swanley, an industrial town, was a tiny village until the railway came in 1861; it still has a small church beneath a grove of pines overlooking the green.

This former agricultural village, swamped by Thames-side industry, has a partly Saxon church tower. An important palaeolithic skull ('Swanscombe Man' or, more correctly, 'Woman') was found in 1935 in an old gravel pit, now the site of a nature reserve.

The village is a scatter of houses along a main road on the windy chalk uplands above Folkestone.

Scores of colourful free-flying butterflies from all over the world are housed in a tropical greenhouse garden among exotic plants such as bougainvillea, oleander and banana. The temperate section is home to British butterflies, with many favourite species and some rarer varieties.
Open late Mar–early Nov daily.

This is a residential extension of Whitstable, suburban in appearance, with a grassy promenade along the clifftop, undercliff and beach huts facing a pleasant shingle beach.

STURRY
VILLAGE ON A28, 3 MILES (5KM) NE OF CANTERBURY

SUNDRIDGE
VILLAGE OFF A25, 3 MILES (5KM) W OF SEVENOAKS

SUTTON AT HONE
VILLAGE ON A225, 3 MILES (5KM) S OF DARTFORD

SUTTON VALENCE
VILLAGE ON A274, 4 MILES (6.5KM) NW OF HEADCORN

SWANLEY
TOWN ON B258, 4 MILES (6.5KM) SW OF DARTFORD

SWANSCOMBE
TOWN OFF A226, 3 MILES (5KM) W OF GRAVESEND

SWINGFIELD MINNIS
VILLAGE ON A260, 5 MILES (8KM) N OF FOLKESTONE

The Butterfly Centre
MCFARLANES GARDEN CENTRE (ON A260 BY JUNCTION WITH ELHAM-LYDDEN ROAD) TEL: 01303 844244

TANKERTON
DISTRICT E OF WHITSTABLE

TEMPLE EWELL
SUBURB OFF A256, 3 MILES
(5KM) NW OF DOVER

Set in the Dour Valley, and once the property of the Knights Templar, Temple Ewell is now a suburban extension of Dover. The church contains panels of 17th-century Swiss glass.

TENTERDEN
SMALL TOWN ON A28,
10 MILES (16KM) SW OF
ASHFORD

This is a delightful old town above Rother Levels which grew rich on wool and weaving in the Middle Ages. The broad High Street has stylish shops, especially antiques shops, in fine half-timbered houses which were built in the prosperous weaving days, and elegant 18th-century buildings from its days as an agricultural market town. The church, founded in 1180, has a magnificent 15th-century tower, 125ft (38m) high.

Tenterden & District Museum
STATION RD (OFF A28)
TEL: 01580 764310

The buildings and history of Tenterden, the Cinque Ports and the Weald of Kent are featured at this local history museum. There are corporation records and insignia as well as exhibits on local trades, agriculture and hop growing. Also on display here is the Tenterden Tapestry.
    Open Apr–Oct, most afternoons; Mar wknd afternoons only.

THANET, ISLE OF
AREA IN NE KENT,
CONTAINING MARGATE AND
RAMSGATE

The north-east corner of Kent, including the North Foreland, was a true island well into historical times, but the old strait is now Minster and Chislet Marshes.

**THROWLEY AND THROWLEY
FORSTAL**
HAMLETS OFF A251,
4 MILES (6.5KM) SW OF
FAVERSHAM

Hidden among the Kentish cherry orchards of the North Downs, Throwley is a scatter of farms, but Throwley Forstal is a small cluster grouped about its green.

TONBRIDGE
TOWN OFF A21, 6 MILES
(9.5KM) SE OF SEVENOAKS

This pleasant old town is dominated by the 13th-century gatehouse of a Norman castle demolished in the Civil War, and now surrounded by landscaped gardens. The town has spread along the road away from the River Medway, spanned by a Victorian cast-iron bridge, and the northern part of the High Street has many attractive 18th- and 19th-century buildings. The famous school was founded in 1553.

TROTTISCLIFFE
VILLAGE OFF A20, 1 MILE
(1.5KM) N OF WROTHAM
HEATH

Pronounced 'Trosley', this is an old village of weatherboarded houses just beneath the North Downs, with a fascinating church including parts of a former palace of the bishops of Rochester. Nearby Trosley Country Park covers 160 acres (65ha) of downland, and includes three waymarked paths, one to Coldrum Stones, and a neolithic long barrow excavated in 1910 to reveal 22 skeletons.

This cheerful former spa town grew up amid the Wealden forests after Lord North discovered its chalybeate spring in 1606. Until that time there were only a few scattered cottages and farms hereabouts, so Tunbridge Wells has no medieval or Tudor buildings. The initial visitors roughed it in cottages, lodged in nearby towns or, like Queen Henrietta Maria, camped out on the common.

Building began in 1638 when a grassy promenade, called the Walk, was laid out beside the medicinal spring and visitors 'took the waters' in the morning and socialised afterwards. Later, the Walk was paved with square earthenware tiles, giving rise to its present name, the Pantiles.

Tunbridge Wells grew haphazardly and informally, and is a very attractive town, its charm arising from 18th- and 19th-century elegance including Decimus Burton's Calverley Park and Calverley Park Terrace, and the buildings on Mount Sion and Mount Ephrahim. The common is a superb open space, while the most famous area, the Pantiles, is in effect an 18th-century shopping precinct: a raised paved walkway shaded by lime trees, and fronted by shops behind a colonnade, which gives uniformity to otherwise varied architecture.

TUNBRIDGE WELLS
TOWN ON A26, 31 MILES (50KM) SE OF LONDON

The Pantiles, a tree-lined promenade, is at the heart of Tunbridge Wells

Tunbridge Wells Museum & Art Gallery
CIVIC CENTRE, MOUNT PLEASANT
TEL: 01892 526121 & 547221

The museum displays local and natural history, archaeology, toys and dolls, and domestic and agricultural bygones. There is a fine display of Tunbridge ware. The art gallery has regularly changing exhibitions which include showings of the Ashton Bequest of Victorian oil paintings.
Open all year, daily. Closed Sun, BHs & Etr Sat.

TUNSTALL
VILLAGE ON B2163, 1 MILE (1.5KM) SW OF SITTINGBOURNE

This is a pretty village-cum-suburb of Sittingbourne among the Kentish orchards, with some old houses and a restored 14th-century church.

ULCOMBE
VILLAGE OFF A20, 3 MILES (5KM) SW OF HARRIETSHAM

The scattered village lies on ragstone hills among orchards and hopfields. It ascends a hill along the road to the church with panoramic Wealden views and a huge churchyard yew.

UPCHURCH
VILLAGE OFF A2, 4 MILES (6KM) E OF GILLINGHAM

A little place amid orchards on the edge of the muddy creeks of the Medway estuary, Upchurch has a large early 14th-century church where Sir Francis Drake's father was vicar.

UPNOR, UPPER AND LOWER
VILLAGES OFF A228, 2 MILES (3KM) NE OF STROOD

These Medway villages have a church built in 1878, a flourishing yacht club and an Elizabethan gun station, Upnor Castle.

Upnor Castle
(ON UNCLASS ROAD OFF A228)
TEL: 01634 718742

This attractive turreted castle (English Heritage) stands in a peaceful spot backed by wooded hills on the banks of the River Medway. It was built in 1561 looking across Upnor Reach to the Royal Naval Dockyards, Chatham, intended to guard them. At this it was singularly unsuccessful, for in 1667 the Dutch sailed past the castle, destroyed half the English fleet and sailed back unharmed.
Open Apr–Oct, daily.

WALLAND MARSH
SCENIC REGION NW OF LYDD

Situated to the west of Romney Marsh, this wide stretch of marshland between New Romney, Appledore and Rye was reclaimed in medieval times.

WALMER
DISTRICT OFF A258, IMMEDIATELY S OF DEAL

There are plenty of Victorian houses as well as 20th-century ones in this residential seaside place that merges north up the coast with Deal. Notable buildings include two churches, one Norman, the other Victorian, and ruins of a semi-fortified Norman house beside the old churchyard. On the promenade, Walmer Castle (English Heritage), one of Henry VIII's gun stations, has been the official residence of Lord Warden of the Cinque Ports since the 18th century.

Pleasure boats moored at Wateringbury on the River Medway

The pleasant brewing village of Wateringbury lies among hopfields and orchards of the Medway Valley, with attractive houses, both old and new.

The village, a scatter of big houses, an early Norman church and the lovely Kentish cricket ground at Farleigh Green, is situated among orchards and hopfields beside the River Medway.

This large village has a wide High Street, where most buildings are scheduled for architectural interest. It includes plenty of fine 18th-century façades and 600-year-old Ford House. St Mary's Abbey incorporates parts of a nunnery founded in 1090; St Leonard's Tower is the remains of a Norman manor house; the Tudor Swan Hotel, in Swan Street, was a coaching inn where Dr Johnson stayed.

The fine early Norman tower (English Heritage) is all that remains of a castle or fortified manor house built in about 1080 by Gundulf, Bishop of Rochester.
     Open Apr–Oct, daily.

WATERINGBURY
VILLAGE ON A26, 5 MILES (8KM) W OF MAIDSTONE

WEST FARLEIGH
VILLAGE ON B2010, 3 MILES (5KM) SW OF MAIDSTONE

WEST MALLING
VILLAGE ON A20, 5 MILES (8KM) W OF MAIDSTONE

St Leonard's Tower
ON UNCLASS ROAD W OF A228

WEST PECKHAM
VILLAGE OFF A26, 5 MILES (8KM) NE OF TONBRIDGE

Cottages, a manor farm, an inn and a church form a tight cluster near the village cricket green among the Kentish orchards.

WESTBROOK
DISTRICT OFF A28, W EXTENSION OF MARGATE

This residential suburb of Margate has a famous sea-bathing hospital which was founded in 1791 by Dr Lettsom, founder of the British Medical Society.

WESTENHANGER
VILLAGE OFF A20, 3 MILES (5KM) NW OF HYTHE

Situated beside Folkestone Racecourse, the village is strewn along the Roman Canterbury—Lympne road. Near by is the ruinous fragment of a 14th-century manor house, similar to Bodiam Castle.

WESTERHAM
SMALL TOWN ON A25, 5 MILES (8KM) W OF SEVENOAKS

This pleasant town is set on a rise beneath the Kentish sandstone hills close to the M25. Its High Street, the busy A25, twists over the hill, broadening past the little green to form the old market place, fronted by two former coaching inns. The church, on the northern corner of the green, has an unusual staircase to the tower. The tapering green is surrounded by attractive 17th- and 18th-century houses and dominated by two statues of famous Westerham men. One is a seated likeness of Sir Winston Churchill by Oscar Nemon (1969), the other shows General Wolfe, brandishing his sword.

There are several fine houses in the area, including Quebec House and Squerryes Court.

Quebec House
OFF A25
TEL: 01892 890651

Westerham was the birthplace of General James Wolfe who spent his childhood in the multi-gabled, square brick house now renamed Quebec House (National Trust). The house probably dates from the 16th century but was extended and altered in the 17th century. An exhibition on the Battle of Quebec (1759), housed in Tudor stable block, covers the campaign and the parts played by Wolfe and the Marquis de Montcalm.

Open Apr—Oct, some afternoons.

Squerryes Court
TEL: 01959 562345 & 563118

This beautiful manor house, built in 1681, was acquired by the Wardes in 1731 and is still their family home. It contains important pictures (including many Italian, 17th-century Dutch and 18th-century English paintings), furniture, porcelain and tapestries, all collected by the family in the 18th century. Also on display are items relating to General James Wolfe of Quebec, a family friend, who received his first commission at Squerryes. The lovely garden was landscaped in the 18th century and has a lake, dovecote, and a restored formal garden.

Open Apr—Sep, certain afternoons. Mar, Sun only.

*g*azetteer

This family resort is on the north Kent coast and has a clean, sandy beach backed by chalk cliffs with a grassy clifftop.

This seaside resort on the north Kent coast is famed for its oysters, introduced into the area by the Romans. Whitstable has late 18th-early 19th-century houses at Island Wall and Middle Wall by a 7 mile (11km) shingle beach, and a harbour devoted to yachting and fishing.

Set on the banks of the River Little Stour near a tall, weatherboarded watermill, this attractive village has a triangular-shaped green overhung by big lime and chestnut trees. Characterful buildings stand around the green and in Gutter Street. The late 14th-century church, restored in 1878, has a colourful art nouveau window by Arild Rosencrantz.

WESTGATE ON SEA
DISTRICT OFF A28, ON W OUTSKIRTS OF MARGATE

WHITSTABLE
TOWN ON A290, 6 MILES (10KM) NW OF CANTERBURY

WICKHAMBREAUX
VILLAGE OFF A257, 5 MILES (8KM) E OF CANTERBURY

The pub in Wickhambreaux

This old village, which feels more like a town, stands on the Canterbury–Sandwich road. The church with its tall, green spire and famous Oxinden family monument, stands close to a row of half-timbered buildings, including the Old Canonry at a right-angle bend in the road. The spacious and attractive High Street, with grass verges and pollarded lime trees, is lined with handsome Tudor and Georgian houses. Wingham Bird Park is near by.

WINGHAM
VILLAGE ON A257, 6 MILES (9.5KM) E OF CANTERBURY

WITTERSHAM
VILLAGE ON B2082, 4 MILES (6KM) S OF TENTERDEN

Known as the 'capital' of the Isle of Oxney, this big old village is 214ft (65m) above the Rother Levels. The nearby Stocks windmill (1781) is the tallest post mill in Kent.

WOODCHURCH
VILLAGE OFF B2067, 4 MILES (6KM) E OF TENTERDEN

Grouped around a large green, this is a big friendly village with weatherboarded and timber houses, a noble church with a very tall spire, and a working white smock mill of 1820.

WOULDHAM
VILLAGE OFF A2, 3 MILES (5KM) SW OF ROCHESTER

The village, which has an interesting old church, is set beside the tidal River Medway and surrounded by marshes and overgrown chalk pits. Medieval Starkey Castle Farm is to the north.

WROTHAM
VILLAGE OFF M20, 8 MILES (13KM) N OF TONBRIDGE

This ancient village, pronounced 'Root-em', lies beneath the steep tree-clad slopes of the North Downs, and manages to keep its identity despite nearby motorways (the M20 and M26). The lovely little village

square has an Elizabethan manor house on one side and a 14th- to 15th-century church on the other. The remains of an archbishop's palace are close to the church and the attractive High Street runs off westwards. There is footpath access, including part of the North Downs Way, to Wrotham Water (National Trust) which lies between the village and Trottiscliffe.

The old market town on the North Downs is famed for its agricultural college of London University. There are pleasant Georgian houses in the old part of town near the 15th-century collegiate church, as well as older half-timbered buildings. Wye College occupies the buildings of a college of priests founded in 1447, while 18th-century Olantigh Hall is a venue for the popular summer music festivals. To the south-east, on the escarpment of Wye Downs, is a nature reserve which covers 250 acres (101ha).

WYE
TOWN OFF A28, 4 MILES (6.5KM) NE OF ASHFORD

Enjoy the wonderful views from the Devil's Kneading Trough on Wye Downs

LISTINGS

CONTACTS AND ADDRESSES

USEFUL ADDRESSES AND NUMBERS

National Trust, Scotney Castle, Lamberhurst
Tel: 01892 890651

English Heritage, 1 High Street, Tonbridge
Tel: 01732 778000

TOURIST INFORMATION CENTRES

Ashford, 18 The Churchyard
Tel: 01233 629165

Broadstairs, 6b High Street
Tel: 01843 862242

Canterbury, 34 St Margarets Street
Tel: 01227 766567

Clacket Lane (M25) Eastbound
Tel: 01959 565063

Clacket Lane (M25) Westbound
Tel: 01959 565615

Cranbrook*, Vestry Hall, Stone Street
Tel: 01580 712538

Dartford, The Clocktower, Suffolk Road
Tel: 01322 343243

Deal, Town Hall, High Street
Tel: 01304 369576

Dover, Townwall Street
Tel: 01304 205108

Faversham, Fleur de Lis Heritage Centre, 13 Preston Street
Tel: 01795 534542

Folkestone, Harbour Street
Tel: 01303 258594

Gravesend, 10 Parrock Street
Tel: 01474 337600

Herne Bay, 12 William Street
Tel: 01227 361911

Hythe*, En Route Travel Building, Red Lion Square
Tel: 01622 267799

Maidstone, The Gatehouse, The Old Palace Gardens, Mill Street
Tel: 01622 602169

Margate, 22 High Street
Tel: 01843 220241

New Romney*, Town Hall House, 35 High Street
Tel: 01797 364044

Ramsgate, 19 Harbour Street
Tel: 01843 583333

Rochester, 95 High Street
Tel: 01634 843666

Sevenoaks, Buckhurst Lane
Tel: 01732 450305

Tenterden*, Town Hall, High Street
Tel: 01580 763572

Tonbridge, Tonbridge Castle, Castle Street
Tel: 01732 770929

Tunbridge Wells, The Old Fish Market, The Pantiles
Tel: 01892 515675

Whitstable, 7 Oxford Street
Tel: 01227 275482

Denotes seasonal opening only

CALENDAR OF EVENTS

JANUARY
New Year's Day Revels
Museum of Kent Life,
Cobtree, Lock Lane, Sandling

New Year's Day Treasure Trail
Leeds Castle, Leeds

FEBRUARY
Boat Jumble
The Historic Dockyard, Chatham

MARCH
Dover Film Festival
Town Hall, High Street, Dover

Spring Gardens Week
Leeds Castle, Leeds

APRIL
Medieval Fair
Groombridge Place Gardens,
Groombridge Place,
Groombridge, Tunbridge Wells

A Celebration of Easter
Leeds Castle, Leeds

Chaucer Festival – Spring
Pilgrimage
High Street and Westgate
Gardens, Canterbury

St Georges Day Celebrations
Museum of Kent Life,
Cobtree, Lock Lane, Sandling

MAY
May Day Celebrations
Hever Castle and Gardens,
Hever

Rochester Sweeps Festival
Various venues,
Rochester

Weald of Kent Craft Fair
Penshurst Place and Gardens,
Penshurst

May Day Celebrations
Museum of Kent Life,
Cobtree, Lock Lane, Sandling

Whitstable May Day
Celebrations
Whitstable Castle, Tower Hill,
Whitstable

A Festival of English Food
and Wine
Leeds Castle, Leeds

Sandwich River Festival
North Bank of River Stour,
Adjacent to Old Toll Bridge,
Sandwich

Ramsgate Spring Festival
Various venues, Ramsgate

Dover International Model Boat
Show
Marine Parade, Dover Harbour,
Dover

Merrie England Weekend
Hever Castle and Gardens, Hever

Spring Fayre and Flower Festival
The Friars, Aylesford Friary,
Aylesford

Classic Car Show
Penshurst Place and Gardens,
Penshurst

Festival of Dover: Spirit of
the Sea
Various venues,
Dover

Dickens Festival
Various venues, Rochester

JUNE
Vintage and Veteran Steam and
Transport Rally
Wings of the Morning Field, Top
of Wrotham Hill, Wrotham

Balloon and Vintage Car Fiesta
Leeds Castle, Leeds

Model Railway Exhibition
The Historic Dockyard, Chatham

Battle of Groombridge
Groombridge Place Gardens,
Groombridge Place,
Groombridge, Tunbridge Wells

Broadstairs Dickens Festival
Various venues, Broadstairs

Midsummer Music Festival
Museum of Kent Life,
Cobtree, Lock Lane, Sandling

Sevenoaks Summer Festival
Various venues, Sevenoaks

Stour Music
Boughton Aluph Church,
Boughton Aluph

Chaucer Festival
Various venues, Canterbury

Heavy Horse Day
The Historic Dockyard, Chatham

Leeds Castle Annual Open Air
Concert

LISTINGS

JULY
Swale Festival
Various venues, Sittingbourne,
Faversham and Isle of Sheppey

Hythe Festival Week
Various venues, Hythe

Leeds Castle Annual Open Air
Concert
Leeds Castle, Leeds

Ships Open Days
Royal Harbour, Ramsgate

Elizabethan Entertainment
Penshurst Place and Gardens,
Penshurst

The Kent Event
Museum of Kent Life,
Cobtree, Lock Lane, Sandling

Kent County Show
Showground, Detling

Balloon Fiesta
Penshurst Place and Gardens,
Penshurst

Whitstable Regatta
Tankerton Slopes, Marine Parade,
Whitstable

Ashford International Festival
Various venues, Ashford

Georgian Festivities – Pleasures
On The Pantiles
Pantiles, Royal Tunbridge Wells

Deal Summer Music Festival
Various venues, Deal

AUGUST
South East Garden Festival
The Historic Dockyard,
Chatham

Broadstairs Folk Week
Various venues, Broadstairs

Victorian Fair and Steam Special
The Historic Dockyard,
Chatham

Sheerness Show
Seafront, Sheerness

Norman Rochester
Various venues, Rochester

Finchcocks Festival
Finchcocks, Goudhurst

Faversham Hop Festival
Town Centre, Faversham

Shepway Festival
The Leas, Folkestone

Canterbury International Kite
Festival
Merton Farm, Merton Lane,
Canterbury

SEPTEMBER
Rare Breeds Show and
Country Fair
South of England Rare Breeds
Centre, Highlands Farm,
Woodchurch

Shepway Airshow
The Leas, Folkestone

Weald of Kent Craft Fair
Penshurst Place and Gardens,
Penshurst

Hop Hoodening
Canterbury Cathedral,
Canterbury

Beer and Hop Festival
Museum of Kent Life,
Cobtree, Lock Lane, Sandling

Steam Fair
Civic Centre Car Park, Rochester

Sea Shanty Festival
Various venues, Deal

Leeds Castle Flower Festival
Leeds Castle, Leeds

OCTOBER
Autumn Drama Season
Trinity Theatre and Arts Centre,
Church Road,
Royal Tunbridge Wells

Finchcocks Fair
Finchcocks, Goudhurst

Kent Cider and Apple Festival
Museum of Kent Life,
Cobtree, Lock Lane, Sandling

Canterbury Festival
Various venues, Canterburry

NOVEMBER
Bonfire Night Family Party
Museum of Kent Life,
Cobtree, Lock Lane, Sandling

Grand Fireworks Spectacular
Leeds Castle, Leeds

Winter Wonderland Illuminated
Carnival
Town Centre, Deal, Dover and
Sandwich

DECEMBER
Christmas at The Castle
Leeds Castle, Leeds

Dickensian Christmas
Various Venues, Rochester

Christmas at Cobtree
Museum of Kent Life,
Cobtree, Lock Lane, Sandling

INDEX

INDEX

ACKNOWLEDGEMENTS

The Automobile Association wishes to thank the following photographers and libraries for their assistance in the preparation of this book.

SPECTRUM COLOUR LIBRARY 79
The remaining photographs are held in the Association's own library, (AA PHOTO LIBRARY) and were taken by P Baker 17, 31, 32, 38/9, 66, 77; V & S Bates 34; D Forss 6/7, 15, 28, 41, 49, 50, 52, 57, 62, 63, 65, 69, 73, 85, 87; A Hopkins 90/1; S & O Matthews 10/1, 24, 36, 47, 54, 60/1, 64, 81; J Miller 59; D Noble 22, 44, 76; T Souter 9; R Strange 12, 20/1, 43, 74, 82, 89; W Voysey 18, 70; H Williams 8.

Cover photographs

INTERNATIONAL PHOTOBANK: back – middle
MICHAEL BUSSELLE'S PHOTOLIBRARY: back – top
P BAKER: back – bottom
ZEFA PICTURES LTD: front – main
Steve Watkins/Natural Exposure: front (cyclists)